JOURNEY
INTO
WHOLENESS

JOURNEY
INTO
WHOLENESS

STEPHEN MANLEY

Cross Style Press

JOURNEY INTO WHOLENESS
© 2018 by Stephen Manley

First Published 1983
Revised Edition 1996
Second Revised Edition 2018

Published by Cross Style Press
Lebanon, Tennessee
CrossStyle.org

Edited by Delphine Manley

ISBN-10: 0-9987265-4-0
ISBN-13: 978-0-9987265-4-0

Printed in the United States of America.

CrossStyle.org

CONTENTS

Foreword   7

Acknowledgments   9

1. Fragmented Christianity   11

2. The Light Which Gives Light To Every Man   15

3. Of God the Free Gift   27

4. His Workmanship, Created in Christ   37

5. Inclinations of the Flesh   55

6. Freedom in the Spirit   69

7. The Unfolding Presence of Christ   87

8. Prize of the High Calling   97

Notes   103

FOREWARD

In these pages, Stephen Manley shares with us the gleanings of his study and observations concerning the reality of redemption. He probes the depths of inner-life experience as contrasted with a nominal commitment and an intellectual acquiescence to doctrine. He stresses an all-too-frequently neglected aspect of conversion life, in what he correctly terms "a Christian's progress," which is from prevenient grace, to repentance, to conversion, to initial sanctification, and on to entire sanctification, and finally to glorification.

From the outset, there is set before us the scriptural criterion for vital Christian experience, so succinctly yet beautifully expressed in 2 Corinthians 3:18, "But we all, with unveiled face, beholding as in a mirror the glory of the Lord, are being transformed into the same image from glory to glory, just as by the Spirit of the Lord."

The premise of all eight chapters is the completeness of God's plan of redemption: "that you may stand perfect and complete in all the will of God." (Colossians 4:12). Christian experience is not a series of segregated events; it is integrality, wholeness. We tend to compartmentalize and fragmentize religious experience when it is one expanding miracle of grace: as the author says, "the unfolding presence of Christ." God's plan of redemption is no halfway measure; it is an all-encompassing experience. That concept is expressed in Colossians 1:28: "That we may present everyone perfect in Christ" (NIV). It is also forcefully highlighted in Hebrews 7:25, "Therefore He is also able to save to the uttermost those who come to God through Him, since He always lives to make intercession for them." That is the theme of this book: the restoration of our lost estate.

Evangelist Manley's book has depth aplenty, but it is not dull or tedious reading. On the contrary, it is easy to read, and stimulating withal. It is not a warming over or stereotyped expression, but it is refreshing in its insights and its down-to-earth manner of presenting profound truth. No minister or layperson can read it with open heart and mind and fail to be immensely benefited spiritually.

— **William M. Greathouse**

ACKNOWLEDGMENTS

No man is self-made, especially a man who is in search for truth. No man can say he has alone shaped the truth of his own form, but that he has been shaped by the truth as God has presented it through the Body of Christ around him. Such a man is this evangelist.

Indebted I stand to the congregations that taught me when I was their pastor-teacher. I could not thank enough the numerous individuals in congregations across this land who patiently waited for this evangelist to learn more of the truth they needed to hear.

I am in great obligation to my wife and children who have put home on wheels in order to provide the love and companionship which shapes a man. How can one pay such a debt?

Dr. Kenneth Swan of the English Department of Taylor University would not be paid and could not be adequately paid for his contribution to this writing. It was under his careful guidance that this book took its form and is presented to you.

— **Stephen Lee Manley**

1

FRAGMENTED CHRISTIANITY

The hour of specialization is upon us. In fact, we are specialized to death! In every area of our lives we have been segmented, divided, and segregated. I go to one doctor only to be sent to another, because my ailment is not his specialty. I go to the grocery store and ask where I will find dog food. The clerk says, "I don't know. That is not my department."

In the church, the whole man can receive total ministry. The term "holiness" can rightly be defined as "wholeness." Yet as I look back over my personal experience in the church, I am aware that for a long time my Christianity was departmentalized into sections of experience and doctrine which read like the sections of the local newspaper. What I needed was to see how the parts of the puzzle fit together into the whole. I could talk long and loudly about various aspects of the gospel which seemed important, but each aspect was a segmented section that seemed to have little relationship to the whole. After being raised in the church, after college and formal education for the ministry, and after the continual study necessary in the pastoral ministry, I gradually became aware that I did not have the insight which made Christianity one balanced operation in my life. Because I have traveled in evangelism for a number of years, I have discovered that I am not alone. Many people have their pet doctrine about which they are an authority, but their lives are unbalanced and dissatisfying. Many look at the holiness movement as just one more group with a favorite bias. But I am not interested in pet doctrines. I want a balanced Christianity that produces a whole, integrated living experience. While on earth, Christ was a man living a balanced life. He was without sin. Our Lord did not have the prejudice which blinded the Pharisees. They were narrow, legalistic, and incomplete. Consequently, they shut their world out. Jesus embraced His world in love. He ate with publicans and sinners while unhappy Pharisees looked through the window spewing criticism.

As I look back in my life, I see clearly that the days when I was most pharisaical were the days when my theology was most segmented. I would latch on to one law and harangue critically about everything that was slightly different from it, unable to see the balance in the total law of God. In my attempt to be righteous in one area, I unconsciously missed Christ's likeness in dozens of others.

I have always been hardest on people who reflected my own faults. Like the elder brother in the story of the prodigal son, I have criticized people whose faults made me feel uncomfortable. The elder brother accused the wayward boy being "with harlots" (Luke 15:30). The story does not report that as one of the prodigal's sins although the boy never denied it. Perhaps the elder brother was expressing his own greatest temptation.

I was driven by a great sense of need to stand back and take an overall view of Christianity. Life in Christ should be a journey to wholeness. Most certainly there will be segments of doctrine that are important to analyze and describe, but are these segments separate entities? Should there not be a common element so strong that all parts can be seen as one? So strong, in fact, that the segment cannot be properly understood without the whole?

In seeking the common element, another problem could arise: exchanging one bias for another! I wanted to avoid this, somehow gaining an understanding of the whole of Christianity as *man and God reconciled*. There may be various stages of growth, various aspects of divine intervention, and various crisis experiences. But when it is all said and done, the beauty of Christianity unfolds at every point and stage of growth as man and God are reconciled to each other.

Paul expressed it well: "Therefore, if anyone is in Christ, he is a new creation; old things have passed away; behold, all things have become new. Now all things are of God, who has reconciled us to Himself through Jesus Christ..." (2 Corinthians 5:17-19). He states further that since we have been reconciled, we have been given the "ministry of reconciliation," and we have had committed to us the "word of reconciliation."

Once this truth grips a person's heart and mind, it is not hard to see unity in every page of the Word of God. God's purpose for man from the beginning was intimacy. He created Adam and Eve in His image, to be "partakers of the divine nature" (2 Peter 1:4). His desire for man was personal fellowship. This design has not changed. When sin brought the chasm between God and man, God immediately moved to bridge that gulf. His purpose for doing so was to restore man to His image, to restore the fellowship that man and God had enjoyed.

Here then is the uniting thread that ties every element of Christian experience together the work of *reconciliation*. Reconciliation is the act of bringing two estranged parties back together, to reestablish the relationship. All the laws of God point in one direction toward fellowship with Him. The Bible as a whole has one purpose to lead us to *fellowship with God*. Every experience taught in Christian theology must have that one intent.

Is there anything higher than man in intimate fellowship with his God? Is anything of great value? We have found the key!

So this is the purpose of my journey: to see each segment of the Christian life in the glorious light of fellowship with God. Where do I begin? The story starts with man already in sin and God intervening in his behalf.

2

THE LIGHT WHICH GIVES LIGHT TO EVERY MAN

How sinful is the human race? I see many non-Christians who are better people than some Christians. There is good in every man; all you have to do is find it. Aren't some people just naturally better than others?

All of these questions and comments were raised when I was growing up. Somehow they have always seemed to be right at the heart of what I believe. I have had the feeling that to come up with answers to them would clarify most theological concepts.

What one believes about sin determines what kind of redemption he envisions. If sin is a small rash on a man's skin, then a mere healing cream will be sufficient. But if one is dealing with a disease of the heart that constantly secretes its evil influence into the life, a radical cure is going to be necessary.

We all accept the truth that man was created perfect by God. How else could a perfect God make man?

The Genesis account tells us that man was made in "the

image of God." Wesley teaches that the image of God in the life of a man is twofold. Man is made in the natural image of God, and he is made in God's moral image. The natural image is what makes man a human being. It contains our freedom of will, our ability to reason, our immortality, and our dominion over all things created. These are the elements that make man a man instead of an animal. The second element in the likeness is the moral image of God. This is man's Godlikeness. God is righteousness, holiness, and perfect love. These are the qualities that He placed at the heart, the motivating center of mankind.

Genesis 3 records the most terrible of all tragedies. We call it the Fall. Man went from the high place of his perfection to the low place of his disgrace. When man fell, what happened to him? How far did he fall? The scene was this: A perfect man entered into a tragic sin; a man of total innocence and goodness became a man of total depravity.

Two states of total depravity need to be described, depicted on the chart (see next page) by capital letters and by lowercase letters. If in the Fall, God had left man to his choice, he would have gone into TOTAL DEPRAVITY, a state of complete separation from God. Here he would have lost his capacity to be man. He would have become an animal, driven only by appetites, instincts, and passions. He would have been incapable of wanting God or of doing a good deed. He would have lost his free will.

Wesley asks a series of questions that brings our fallen nature into focus. "Is man by nature filled with all manner of evil? Is he void of all good? Is he wholly fallen? Is his soul totally corrupted? Is every imagination of the thoughts of his heart only evil continually?" Then in a bold statement he declares that if you answer yes to these questions, you are a Christian; but if you deny this, you are still a heathen.[1] This is man totally void of God.

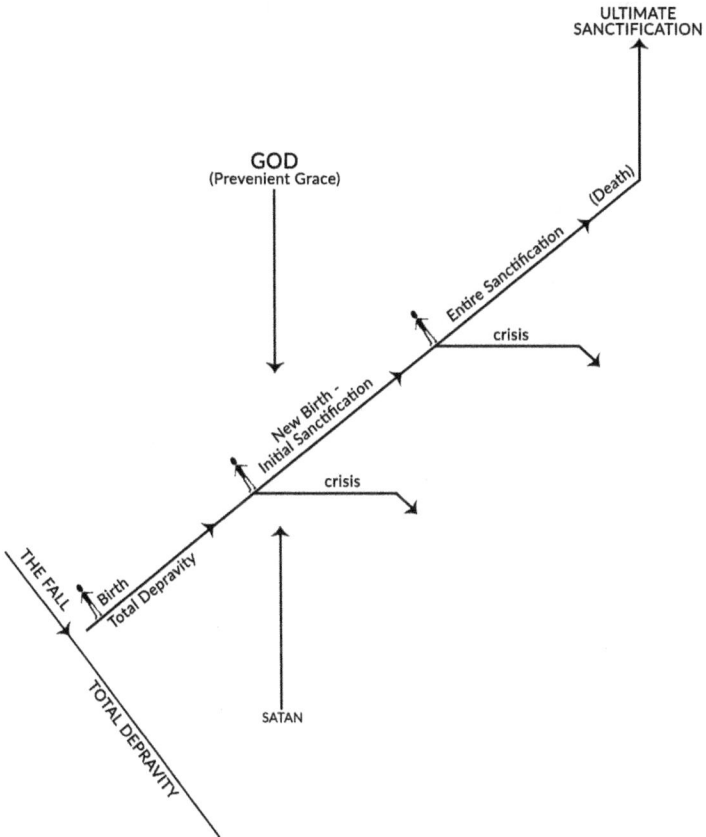

Wesley goes on to state the case even stronger. He writes, "And in Adam all died, all human kind, all the children of man who were then in Adam's loins. The natural consequence of this is that everyone descended from him comes into the world spiritually dead, dead to God, wholly dead in sin; entirely void of the life of God, void of the image of God, of all that righteousness and holiness wherein Adam was created."[2] In this condition man bears the image of the devil in pride and self-will. The condition expresses itself in sensual appetites and desires. Wesley calls it "the image of the beast."

The second state is represented by the Total Depravity shown in the capital and small letters on the ascending line of the chart. Here total depravity means all the areas of man's life have been touched with sin. The image of God is not lost, as in the previous state, but is scarred. In this state man has a free will restored to a degree. He is capable of good deeds but not all good deeds; he has some good thoughts but not all good thoughts. He can again desire God.

What makes the difference between these two states? It is God alone. TOTAL DEPRAVITY, uppercase, is man void of the redeeming touch of God. Depravity, lowercase, is man with God's touch anew. If God had stood back, leaving man totally to his rebellion, he would have ceased to be man. He would have lost totally the natural image of God provided in creation. His situation would have been indescribably hopeless. In his moral image of God, man would have lost every desire for God and righteousness, but God intervened. This intervention is called prevenient grace.

According to H. Orton Wiley, "Prevenient grace, as the term implies, is that grace which 'goes before' or prepares the soul for entrance into the initial state of salvation."[3] Another word for grace is "love." Grace is the expression of God's love. By definition, prevenient grace is all the love of God that comes to a man before he experiences salvation. Even before man responds to God's call, God has showered him with His love! He has spoken to us through nature. He has given us longings to be better than we are. God has convicted us of sin. All of this comes through the touch of prevenient grace.

Wesley proclaims this great truth in his sermon on "Working Out Your Own Salvation." He declares, "Allowing that all the souls of men are dead in sin by nature this excuses none, seeing there is no man that is in the state of mere nature. There is no man, unless he has quenched the Spirit, that is wholly void of the grace of God."[4] In order to sin, a man must go against the grace that God has given to him. Because every man has prevenient grace to a greater or lesser degree, he is without excuse. Wesley indicates that there might be a small number whose consciences are "seared as with a hot iron." But that exception only proves the rule. Every individual has some measure of the "Light, which lighteth every man."

One fact stands absolute. No man is void of this grace in his life. Every man in every generation, of every nation, has this touch of God on him. Wesley used a phrase "free in all, and free for all."[5] In this, Wesley stands opposed to the Calvinistic concept. Wesley's view is a "universal or common grace given to all men, though not the same as Calvin thought. For Calvin, universal grace was for restraining evil operations and for limiting man's uncontrolled fury."[6] Wesley's view of prevenient grace is also opposed to the Calvinistic concept of limited grace that grace is given only to persons how are the elect specially selected by God. Wesley proposed that prevenient grace is for "everyone who dwells upon the face of the earth," and it is free for all in the sense that God gives it without price; "he confers it on a sinner in the very state of his sinfulness."[7] Everyone receives God's gift of prevenient grace which "waiteth not for the call of any man" but is universally given. There are none who are without it; "Christians, Mohammedans, pagans, the vilest of savages, all possess some measure of preventing grace."[8]

However, we must never be satisfied to read just what the great theologians have thought. What does God's Word say about prevenient grace? The word *prevenient* comes from theology and not from the biblical text; it is nonetheless a biblical concept, woven into the fabric of the entire Word of God. The concepts of justification, regeneration, and sanctification all presuppose prevenient grace.

John 1:9 says, "That was the true Light which gives light to every man coming into the world." Most commentators explain this verse as referring to Christ and His impact on the world. However, Wesley adds an interesting viewpoint in his *Explanatory Notes upon the New Testament*, where he comments that the light "which gives light to every man coming into the world" is "vulgarly termed natural conscience, pointing out at least the general lines of good and evil. And this light if man did not hinder would shine more and more to the perfect day."[9] What Wesley termed "natural conscience" can properly be called prevenient grace. While the primary reference in John 1:9 is to *more* than natural conscience, both conscience and God's gift of His Son Jesus Christ are acts of His grace.

In John 6:44, Jesus says, "No one can come to Me unless the Father who sent Me draws him; and I will raise him up at the last day." No man can believe on Christ, except God give him power to do so. Man does not believe in order to get God to move upon him. Rather God moves upon man, and man responds by belief. This movement of God which draws us to believe is called prevenient grace.

Though this grace comes from God's power, it is not irresistible. Wesley writes that God works "not by compulsion, not by laying the will under any necessity; but by the strong and sweet, yet still resistible, motions of his heavenly grace."[10]

In John 15:5, our Lord declares, "I am the vine, you are the branches. He who abides in Me, and I in him, bears much fruit; for without Me you can do nothing." There is no possibility of bearing Christian fruit without God's enabling power. The fruit of repentance and belief do not occur apart from Him. Even the fruit of desiring Him is a product of His grace. Everything is traceable back to His initiative and help.

Acts 5:31 says, "Him God has exalted to His right hand to be Prince and Savior, to give repentance to Israel and forgiveness of sins." To give repentance and to give forgiveness are two levels of grace. Man must cooperate in repentance, but Christ alone can forgive sins. Since man cooperates in repentance, it bespeaks a divine movement that makes our cooperation possible. This is prevenient grace.

In Romans 1:19-20 Paul writes, "...because what may be known of God is manifest in them, for God has shown it to them." There is an outward revelation of nature which declares the power of God. Thus every man stands without excuse, having had a revelation of God to his life another action of God's prevenient grace.

Romans 5:6 relates, "For when we were still without strength, in due time Christ died for the ungodly." When we were unable to think, to will, or to do anything good, Christ died and provided in His death a prevenient grace.

Again we read in Romans 5:18, "Therefore, as through one man's offense judgment came to all men, resulting in condemnation, even so through one Man's righteous act the free gift came to all men, resulting in justification of life." Under Adam we all entered into a state of judgment. The only way out for us is to fight against the Adamic nature that we were born with but in the fight man is destined to failure. However, there is good news. Although we have all been born with the Adamic nature, we have also been born under the shadow of God's grace. W.T. Purkiser writes, "Prevenient grace is a pervasive influence that will shepherd him to conversion and sanctification and finally to heaven, unless he determinedly breaks his way out. In Adam it is impossible to be saved. In Christ as are all men potentially it is hard to be lost."[11]

Does not 2 Corinthians 3:5 speak for itself? "Not that we are sufficient of ourselves to think of anything as being from ourselves, but our sufficiency is from God..." Man without God is unable to think a good thought or do a good deed, but God has given prevenient grace.

Paul has been speaking about the power of God which worked in Christ when He was brought forth from the grave. Now he applies it to us. "And you He made alive, who were dead in trespasses and sins..." (Ephesians 2:1). We were dead; we were void of all life. We were incapable of desiring or moving in a spiritual direction except for His quickening. Was not the beginning of His quickening in our lives prevenient grace?

In Ephesians 2:8 we read, "For by grace you have been saved through faith, and that not of yourselves; it is the gift of God..." Grace is the beginning and the end of our relationship with God. Here Paul strikes at the heart of selfish pride. We have no goodness of ourselves. From the initial movement to the last step, all our goodness is of Him.

"For it is God who works in you both to will and to do for His good pleasure." (Philippians 2:13). What a thought! Wesley says, "The meaning of these words may be made more plain by a small transposition of them: It is God that of his good pleasure works in you both to will and to do. This position of the words, connecting the phrase, 'of his good pleasure,' removes all imagination of merit from man, and gives God the whole glory of his work."[12] If this were not true, man would surely boast about some good thing he had done to merit the divine movement. No, God moved first and that movement is called prevenient grace.

Every man has the touch of God on his life. Titus 2:11 says, "For the grace of God that brings salvation has appeared to all men..." No man is void of prevenient grace, the "Light which gives light to every man" which, if followed, will lead him to repentance and the forgiveness of sins.

From the scriptures which we have quoted, one can draw several conclusions. First is the fact that God has made provision for us regardless of birthplace or cultural setting. Second, every man is without excuse as is shown in Romans 1:19-20. If this is true, it must apply to the heathen who have never heard the gospel preached. One cannot meet a man who is totally untouched by the God who is "not willing that any should perish but that all should come to repentance" (2 Peter 3:9).

Margaret Mead has done research in the islands of the South Pacific. She, along with others, developed a system to study the aboriginal tribes in isolated parts of the world.

The number one and number two questions always asked by these anthropologists are, "What do the people in this tribe believe about God? And what is their concept of right and wrong? Never has there been a tribe located which has not had some idea of a creating God and a system of right and wrong in which deeds are not only punished or rewarded by the tribe but in which one is amenable to a higher law of reward and punishment in the universe.[13] Where do these tribes get their information? It is God's prevenient grace.

Even Calvin himself was forced to be inconsistent with his concept of limited election and irresistible grace. In his prefix to the *French New Testament* he says, "The Lord never left himself without a witness, even toward them unto whom he had not sent any knowledge of his word."[14] Calvin recognized that all creation from the firmament above to the center of the earth are witnesses of the glory of God to all men.

Not only are there these outward revelations of the divine, but if man decides to seek God, he does not have to look far, "for everyone might find Him in his own self."

Will not a man be judged for what he knows, rather than what he does not know? Will not the God of grace expect every man to walk in all the light that he has?

Indeed God has made adequate provision for every man through prevenient grace.

Imagine that a man has just come into the courtroom of God. He is pleading to be allowed entrance into heaven. His appeal is based on his own goodness. He has gone to church, raised a good family, and paid his debts. Do you see the weakness of such an appeal? How could a man stand before God and claim any goodness as his own, when God alone enabled him to have goodness? The good deed that even the non-Christian does is a result of prevenient grace. All goodness anyplace at any time comes from God. No man has the right to credit his righteousness to himself.

Some have thought that repentance and faith were works one could do in order to get God to move upon his life. If this were the case, repentance would be a good work which earns God's approval. Thus man could take pride in starting the salvation process. But prevenient grace settles that issue. Works of repentance are a result of God's gift. They come from grace, not from the natural ability of man. One does not repent in order to get God to move; God has moved and man responds to that movement by repentance. Man cooperates with the divine activity that is present in his life. "Grace is not the irresistible power of God over-coming the will of man, but it is the loving hand of a Father enabling the child to use the resources given him in the first place by the Father."[15]

When one stands back to view the whole of Christianity, he sees the first step has been taken by God. Man is incapable of moving towards God, but God has intervened. If the total thrust of Christianity is man and God reconciled, it is settled once and for all that reconciliation is of God. The fountain from which all Christian doctrines and experiences flow is from the fountain of divine activity — God's prevenient grace, the "Light, which lighteth every man."

Of necessity, God's love for man — His grace extended must draw man to crisis moments. Such a crisis moment is the experience of initial sanctification. We call it the new birth.

3

OF GOD THE FREE GIFT

There is a block of wood in my study which has been there since I began my ministry. It came from a Georgia pine tree and is a constant reminder that the love of God is a free gift. I cut the piece of wood with my own hands, but the tree was given to me. I varnished the souvenir so the grain in the wood could be clearly seen, but I did not place it there. It was all of Him, a free gift.

The idea for this memento came to me from a story of the great saint, Abelard. He had a faithful follower, Thibault. Often they enjoyed long periods of meditation in the forest. God would speak through His Word and through nature, preparing them for the task ahead. During one of these periods they heard a shrill cry. Thibault searched until he found a baby rabbit caught in a snare. Tenderly he cut the snare. As he nestled the rabbit in his arms, it looked up as if to express thanks, and died. Rushing to Abelard, Thibault cried, "Please explain the love of God to me in terms of a dying rabbit." How does God's love apply to one who suffers because of the sin of man?

Abelard thought for a long moment, then pointed to a tree that had fallen. "Do you see the rings that form the grain in that tree? They run the entire length of the trunk, but you see them only at the cross section where they are exposed."

It became clear to Thibault that the love of God runs the entire length of time. The coming of Jesus Christ is the great cross section where that love is exposed. In a lesser sense we repeatedly experience the love of God in crisis moments, but it has been there all the time. The prevenient grace of God has been working continually, but we hadn't seen it.

One of those cross sections of life is called initial sanctification, a moment when one experiences the love of God which has been flowing from the beginning. Initial sanctification is a part of the new birth. Being converted is sanctification in its beginning stage holiness begun. The two parts of initial sanctification are forgiveness (justification) and the new birth. They are not separate experiences, but rather two sides to the one coin of personal salvation. Let us speak of justification first.

Justification is the basis for and beginning of the Christian life. Wesley viewed it as the gate or door to salvation. Forgiveness is preceded by prevenient grace and could never be experienced without it. Justification is a result of man's response to the grace that God initiates.

Wesley gives us the following clear definition: "the plain scriptural notion of justification is pardon, the forgiveness of sins. It is the act of God the Father, whereby for the sake of the propitiation made by the blood of his Son, he 'showeth forth his righteousness (or mercy) by the remissions of sins that are past."[1] It is here that condemnation for sin is removed. Man's sins as recorded in the past have been blotted out and shall be remembered against him no more.

Justification is a legal term. It has to do with an act of God which takes place in the divine courtroom. The justice of God has found a man guilty of voluntary disobedience against God's law. The penalty is severe. But now based upon the atoning work of Christ, the word "Pardon" has been stamped over the record of our sins. This is an act that God does for us; it does not include what He does *in* us.

What is justification? Wesley writes: "It is evident from what has already been observed that it is not the being made actually just and righteous. This is sanctification; which is, indeed, in some degree the immediate fruit of justification, but nevertheless, is a distinct gift of God, and of a totally different nature."[2]

Arminius was also concerned about keeping the righteousness of Christ clear in regard to justification. He believed that justification was an act of God, the Judge, who pronounced man righteous in His sight. But this immediately brings up the problem of imputed righteousness a righteousness that is given by God without any choice or action by us. Indeed the righteousness of Christ is imputed to the believer, but to stop there would be disastrous. Our own righteousness certainly does not cause God to justify us; nor is Christ's righteousness a coat thrown over our unrighteousness. Justification does something for us, so that Christ can do something in us. We are declared righteous before God because He has actually forgiven us. The remission of sins has taken place and one becomes righteous through that forgiveness. What a glorious position to be in!

H. Orton Wiley summarizes it thus: "Justification is the judicial or declarative act of God, by which He pronounces those who believingly accept the propitiatory offering of Christ, as absolved from their sins, released from their penalty, and accepted as righteous before Him."[3]

So we see that God has touched man's life through prevenient grace. When one responds to God's grace in a positive way, it expands in his life. The more light one follows, the more light he gets until sufficient light and obedience bring him to a place of repentance and faith. Salvation (initial sanctification) begins with justification. Man's relation to the law has been changed. He is not made completely righteous in nature but has been pardoned of sin. He has been both forgiven and accepted by God as in a right relationship with the Heavenly Father.

"Who should be justified?" Paul answers: "him who does not work but believes on Him who justifies the ungodly" (Romans 4:5). It is the ungodly who need to be justified. The righteous need no repentance. It is the lost whom Christ came to seek and to save. Justification is thus the provision for the guilty to become guiltless, for the unrighteous to become right with God.

Some may say in their self-righteousness that they are not guilty but have spent their lives in doing good deeds. Wesley deals with this in his sermon on "Justification by Faith": "If it be objected, 'Nay, but a man, before he is justified, may feed the hungry, or clothe the naked; and these are good works;' the answer is easy. He may do these, even before he is justified. And these are, in one sense, 'good works;' they are 'good and profitable to men.' But it does not follow, that they are, strictly speaking, good in themselves or good in the sight of God."[4] The works done before justification are not good in the Christian sense because they do not come from faith in Christ.

When should a man be justified? He should seek God when prevenient grace has brought him to an awareness of his guilt for sin. By faith he can present himself to God as one who is ready to be justified.

Why should I be justified? The answer should be clear by this time. If the total view of Christianity is God and man being reconciled, there must have been something that broke the fellowship. It is sin.

Man was made in the image of God. The Creator gave him a perfect law which he was capable of keeping and he was required to keep it. But Adam did not keep the law, so he fell into sin. By his disobedience sin entered into the world and death came by sin; thus death became the lot of all men. It was at this point that God intervened in our behalf. The first step was to remove the guilt through justification. Paul writes: "Therefore, as through one man's offense judgment came to all men, resulting in condemnation, even so through one Man's righteous act the free gift came to all men, resulting in justification of life" (Romans 5:18).

But the offer of justification is not without a required response. Prevenient grace, when responded to, becomes what might be called "convicting grace." This is the first step toward the door of salvation. Conviction leads to repentance, the next response that must take place in a convicted heart. These are what the Bible calls "fruits worthy of repentance" (Matthew 3:8) which will precede justifying faith.

Wesley relates, "We have received it as a maxim that a man is to do nothing in order to receive justification. Nothing can be more false. Whoever desires to find favor with God should 'cease from evil, and learn to do well.' Whoever repents should 'do works meet for repentance.'"[5] The Scripture, our own common sense, and experience all convince us that we should do these works of repentance. But there is a distinction between works of repentance in order *to attain or find* justification, and works of repentance *to merit or purchase* justification.

In other places Wesley taught the biblical truth that we are justified by faith alone. "Faith is the condition, and the only condition of justification. It is the condition: none is justified but he that believes: without faith no man is justified."[6]

How can these statements be reconciled with the need for repentance? Indeed repentance is necessary, but godly sorrow always must be accompanied by faith. A man may have ever so many works meet for repentance, but he is not justified until he believes. Faith may be preceded and aided by repentance, but in the final analysis the only condition of justification is faith.

Therefore, repentance and faith are not self-works that earn or merit the right of justification. They are responses to the movement of God which has brought the heart to this moment.

A multitude of scriptures could be shared in support of the theme of justification. Let us view the Book of Romans, since justification by faith is the theme of the book.

The first three chapters show the helplessness of our plight. Universal sin is convincingly revealed, first, in the Gentiles, and then in the Jews. Paul climaxes with the all-inclusive statement, "for all have sinned and fall short of the glory of God..." (Romans 3:23).

Now Paul says, "Let me tell you the answer to this plight." He declares the method in Romans 3:21-31. It is justification by faith! Since the sin of man is universal, of necessity this offer of justification must be universal. But do not think for one moment that since it is by faith, the law is destroyed; rather the law is honored.

In Romans chapter 4, Paul portrays Abraham as a convincing illustration of justification by faith. "For what does the Scripture say? 'Abraham believed God, and it was accounted to him for righteousness'" (Romans 4:3). Logic would tell us that he was justified apart from the law because he lived before the law was given. If justification is not by works, or the law, how shall we be justified? Paul replies, "Let me show you Jesus 'who was delivered up because of our offenses, and was raised because of our justification'" (Romans 4:25). It is through faith in this Christ that we are forgiven."

Through the rest of the doctrinal section of Romans, Paul expands the work of justification into the work of sanctification. The righteous position received in justification becomes the righteous nature through the fullness of the Spirit.

The Epistle to the Galatians is also an explanation of the doctrine of justification of faith. After Paul's greeting and introduction, he launches into a vindication of himself and this doctrine.

Beginning at Galatians 2:15, he states the folly of the Jewish Christians leaving justification by faith and returning to the old legalism. Believing in salvation through the law is foolish on the basis of what they have already experienced through justification by faith in Christ. The experience of Abraham also says that it is foolish. If they revert back to the law, they will again be under the curse of the law, and the law has no redeeming power to offer those who disobey it. The law has no power to make any changes in the covenant of justification by faith. It came 430 years after the promise of faith had been given to Abraham. The law was a tool to teach one he could not make it without the intervention of Christ who provided justification by faith.

What one loses when he slips back into legalism, surrendering his justification by faith in Christ, ought to convince any thinking person not to do it. One loses the blessing of his inheritance as a child of God and ends up in bondage to ceremonialism again. He is on the verge of becoming a child of Abraham after the flesh, instead of the child of promise. But worst of all, he loses his spiritual liberty and makes Christ's sacrifices of no avail.

The experience of being justified by faith is never isolated in Scripture, and we should never isolate it in our thinking. It never stands alone. If justification is the gateway into salvation, the minute one passes through that threshold, he confronts the new birth regeneration. These two belong together.

Wesley writes: "If any doctrine within the whole compass of Christianity may be termed fundamental, they are doubtless these two: the doctrine of justification, and that of the new birth: the former relating to that great work which God does for us, in forgiving our sins; the latter, to the great work which God does in us, in renewing our fallen nature."[7]

In our experience, neither of these comes before the

other. They happen simultaneously in the believer. In justification the wrath of God is turned away from the believer. In that moment the Holy Spirit begins His work in our hearts the work of the new birth: man, created anew in Christ.

4

HIS WORKMANSHIP, CREATED IN CHRIST

There Christian experience has as its goal the reconciliation of God and man. God wants His wayward child back in His circle of love. It is God's love before one is saved that does not allow us to be one moment without the pressing influence of God's hand. We have explained that this is prevenient grace: God's initiative that presses us by His love to the awareness of sin. It enables us to respond in repentance and faith so that we enter into the experience of conversion which includes initial sanctification. Thus, the new birth is the fulfillment of the yearning of the heart of God. Reconciliation has taken place; the life of God and the life of man are now interwoven. No greater experience is afforded man than to experience this oneness with God.

Our attention now turns from the courtroom where God's justice is seen, to view His work in the heart of man.

Justification is what God does for us; now we shall see what He does within us. To see the new birth is to view the actual invasion of God into our hearts.

There are those who want to speak of salvation only in terms of justification or forgiveness of sin. They are quite content for God to juggle the record contained in the books of heaven. It is, however, a shallow perception that pictures God as the grandfather of the sky who merely pats His children on the head, making everything alright. The new birth brings an alteration within the life of man.

The very words tell us what this alteration involves. It is a change from death to life. When the soul is absent from the body, the body is dead. When the presence of God is absent from the soul, the soul is dead. This is the heart of the warning that God gave man in the Garden of Eden when He talked to him about sin: "...but of the tree of the knowledge of good and evil you shall not eat, for in the day that you eat of it you shall surely die" (Genesis 2:17). There is no question about it: "The wages of sin is death" (Romans 6:23).

This death is described as the absence of God. John writes: "He who has the Son has life; he who does not have the Son of God does not have life" (1 John 5:12). This life is not simply something that Christ gives to us; it is what He is within us. The new birth in its essence is Christ invading the spirit of man with His Spirit.

Let us illustrate this truth from a human relationship. When two individuals who have been friends become bitter enemies, there needs to be reconciliation. Finally one comes to the other in great sorrow. He apologizes and asks forgiveness. Will the second person reach into his pocket and produce an item called forgiveness? Will both ask for time so they can go downtown to purchase forgiveness? Does reconciliation have substance? No. One individual hugs the other, and they weep together. They are friends again. Forgiveness means reconciliation.

I had the great advantage of being raised in a Christian home. The teachings of Christianity were powerful and clear. Yet there was a key insight that I missed. I understood that God lived in His great sky. Upon the confession of my sins, which I did in every revival, He would send down to me a substance called forgiveness. I would jump up after my confession and cry, "I have got it!" By "it" I meant God's forgiveness.

Later I found myself searching for the other resources that I needed in my life. Power, happiness, life, peace, and forgiveness were all on my list. Many times I blamed God for my failures. If temptation overcame me, it was because God did not give me enough power. What a day when I discovered that God does not give me "things"! He gives me himself. He invades my spirit and wraps His arms around my inner self. God and I become one again. This is the new birth.

There are several words in the New Testament that convey this understanding. The term "born again," which we get from Jesus' conversation with Nicodemus, gives us the concept. Our Lord used the words *gennethe anothen* which literally means "born from above." This shows the action of God in our behalf. Life flows from the person of God to the person of man.

H. Orton Wiley states: "Regeneration must be regarded as that impartation of life to the souls of men, which sets them up as distinct individuals in the spiritual realm.

Evidently our Lord intended by His use of the term 'born from above,' to make a distinction between the prevenient grace which is given to all men, and the mysterious issue of grace in individual regeneration."[1] John's use of the term clearly indicates the new birth as a distinct and complete act. The word for "born" is *ogegennemenos*. It is used in the perfect tense which indicates the completion of a process.

Another word that expresses the new life of God in man is *regeneration*. In Titus 3:5 we read: "...according to His mercy He saved us, through the washing of regeneration and renewing of the Holy Spirit..." The Greek word for regeneration is *palingenesia,* with various meanings: new birth, reproduction, renewal, recreation, moral renovation, regeneration, the production of new life consecrated to God.

In Ephesians 2:5 Paul uses the word "quickened" to tell us of this same experience. Jesus also states in John 5:21, "The Son quickeneth whom he will" (KJV). The Greek word used here is *zoopoiei*. It means "to produce alive, beget or bear living young, to cause to live." What a great description of the coming of the resurrected life of Christ to the heart of man!

Paul states it in yet another way when he writes in 2 Corinthians 5:17, "Therefore, if anyone is in Christ, he is a new creation; old things have passed away; behold, all things have become new."

He continues in one of my favorite verses, Ephesians 2:10, "For we are His workmanship, created in Christ Jesus for good works, which God prepared beforehand that we should walk in them." Wesley comments: "Only the power that makes a world can make a Christian. He has a new life, new senses, new faculties, new affections, new appetites, new ideas, and new conceptions. His whole tenor of action and conversation is new, and he lives as it were in a new world."[2]

Another statement which speaks of this same great experience is that of Paul exhorting us in Ephesians 4:24, "...that you put on the new man which was created according to God, in true righteousness and holiness." In Colossians 3:10 is a parallel passage: "put on the new man who is renewed in knowledge according to the image of Him who created him..." When one puts his faith in Christ, he is declared to be righteous through justification. But at this same moment he is initially sanctified "in true righteousness and holiness." This is the change that takes place within the man. It is so different from mere growth or gradual reformation that Paul refers to it as "the new man."

Wesley writes of this Christian experience:

> It is that great change which God works in the soul, when he brings it into life; when he raises it from the death of sin to the life of righteousness. It is the change wrought in the whole soul by the almighty Spirit of God, when it is 'created anew in Christ Jesus;' when the love of the world is changed into the love of God; pride into humility; passion into meekness; hatred, envy, malice, into sincere, tender, disinterested love for all mankind.[3]

Many of the great men of the church in days gone by have given us striking definitions of regeneration. H. Orton Wiley uses the following simple statement:

"Regeneration is the com-munication of life by the Spirit, to a soul dead in trespasses and sins."[4] John Miley states: "Regeneration is the ground of a new spiritual life, a life in righteousness."[5] Wesley writes: "To be born again, is to be inwardly changed from all sinfulness to all holiness. It is fitly so called, because as great a change then passes on the soul as passes on the body when it is born into the world."[6]

Arminius, a Dutch theologian whom Wesley followed, states that the regenerate man has

> *a mind freed from the darkness and vanity of the world, and illuminated with the true and saving knowledge of Christ and with faith, who has affections that are inflamed with such new desires as agree with divine nature, and as are prepared and fitted for newness of living, who has a will reduced to order, and conformed to the will of God, who has powers and faculties able, through the assistance of the Holy Spirit, to contend against sin, the world and Satan, and to gain the victory over them.[7]*

C.S. Lewis speaks of two kinds of life. Biological life which comes through nature "is always tending to run down and decay so that it can only be kept up by incessant subsidies." This biological life is a type, or symbol of the real life that God wants man to have. But it is "only the sort of resemblance there is between a photo and a place, or a statue and a man." In fact, when an individual experiences the new birth, he will "have gone through as big a change as a statue which changed from being a carved stone to being a real man."[8]

In our discussion of the new birth we are not only interested in proper theology but in practical theology. Practical theology asks, "How will it work in my living?" Here is the key test of its value. What effect will the new birth have in my actions and relationships? How will it be demonstrated?

A natural place to turn for an answer is Wesley's sermon on "The Marks of the New Birth."[9] The simplicity of what he says is most encouraging. The characteristic marks of the new birth are faith, hope and love. This *faith* is certainly more than mere mental assent or intellectual agreement. Rather serving faith begins as an awareness of sin in one's life, then proceeds to assurance and confidence in the work of Christ for our salvation. It is followed by power over sin and an abiding peace. The *hope* which marks this experience can be called "full assurance." It includes the witness of the Spirit that we are the children of God. This security is the foundation of hope and produces great joy. *Love* is the final mark of the new birth. Love for God moves into love for one's neighbor. It is reflected not only in outward works but in inward care.

Power over sin needs further investigation because it has presented a problem in the thinking of many. To introduce the discussion, let me suggest three parts of sin which must be handled.

First, there is the guilt of sin. Man has voluntarily disobeyed God. He stands guilty in the courtroom of divine justice. Through the grace provided by the Cross, he is justified and his guilt is canceled.

The second factor is the power of sin. Man has given in to sin so long that sin has become the master. At first he had a choice to do the evil deed or not. But now he has obeyed the call of sin so often that he is trapped. It is the new birth that breaks the power of sin in his life. God invades man's spirit and gives him new desires. This power comes from the Holy Spirit who breaks the grip of sin in our lives.

The third aspect is original sin which we deal with in the discussion of entire sanctification.

We have discovered that one of the great proofs of the new birth is that man quits the sin business. He does not gradually sin less and less; he stops sinning now. Sin is so opposed to the new life he has received that he no longer participates in it. Wesley writes that babes in Christ are so far perfect as "not to commit sin."[10]

The average person reacts to this strong statement by thinking, but no one is perfect! This brings us to the need of a proper definition of sin. Many individuals define it as "anything less than God." But when we think it through, we discover severe problems with that definition. To say sin is anything less than God would imply that Jesus, when He was on this earth, was a sinner. God is omniscient, all-knowing. There was, however, at least one thing that Jesus did not know. He admitted that He did not know the time of His second coming. This lack of knowledge is less than complete knowledge, and by the above definition would be sin.

By this definition, the angels would also be sinners. God is omnipresent but the angels are not. This definition of sin is just not adequate to understand the teachings of Scripture.

For this reason the holiness movement has followed the great thinkers of the Church who accept a more limited definition: Sin is a voluntary disobedience of a known law of God. When Wesley was asked if this is a proper definition of sin, he replied, "I think it is of all such sin as is imputed to our condemnation. And it is a definition which has passed uncensored in the church for at least fifteen hundred years."[11]

"Genuine sinning is man's refusal of offered grace, and willful continuance in inherited inclinations. It is this only that can bring condemnation, and it is this kind of sinning that is not in the believer."[12] The origin of sin is a rebellious heart. It is a fist shaken in the face of God.

Contrasted with this rebellion against a known law of God is human limitation. Although one does not willfully disobey God, that does not mean he is perfect as God is perfect. There are many other areas of life which may be faulty. The newborn Christian is not perfect in the realm of knowledge. If one does not have perfect knowledge, then he will not have perfect judgment. If he does not have perfect judgment, he cannot possibly perform perfect acts. I bought a calculator because I make so many mistakes in my bank book. I keep insurance on my vehicles because I make mistakes in driving. I am not perfect. But these failures are not voluntary disobedience against God. I am not capable of knowing the total will of God; therefore, I am not capable of doing it. I am not capable of saying the right words to the right person at the right time, every time. I have human limitations.

Every man is held accountable for walking in the light that God has given to him. I cannot judge another person fairly because I do not know what knowledge and light he has. Charity one toward the other gives room for the growth of light and obedience. Christ does not expect the same conduct from a Christian junior or teen as He does from the elder saint of God. But Christ does require all of us to walk in all the light we have, lest we enter into voluntary disobedience.

Sin is also related to the heart motive. One may not be perfect in his actions, and yet his heart be in perfect obedience to Christ. A five-year-old boy was patiently waiting for his father to come home from a long business trip. When his father arrived, the lad bounced with glee and shouted, "Can I help you, Daddy?"

His father asked him for a glass of water, and the lad rushed to the kitchen and got the largest glass he could find. He filled it to overflowing and ran down the hallway, splashing water as he went. Holding the rim of the glass with his right hand, the dirt from his fingers washed off into the water.

Approaching his father in a rush, he smiled widely as he offered him the muddy water. His father looked at the faulty offering with love, thanked the boy, and drank it all.

The lad's service left a lot to be desired, but no one can question his motive of love for his father. We all have some mud in our Christian service. Our activities never match up to a perfect standard, but our heart motive can be love expressed in obedience.

Perhaps this truth can be seen more clearly by looking at a Christian in the midst of temptation. Wesley describes the steps that one goes through in the downward progress from grace to sin.[13]

(1) The believer is filled with conquering faith because he is born of God.

(2) A temptation arises. It may come from the world, the flesh, or the devil.

(3) The Holy Spirit is quick to warn the believer that sin is near. The Spirit urges him to be prayerful.

(4) The believer yields, in some degree, to the temptation. The temptation becomes pleasing to him.

(5) The Holy Spirit is grieved, and the believer is rebuked by the Spirit.

(6) The believer does not heed the voice of God, but listens to the voice of temptation.

(7) The evil desire, now yielded to, spreads failure in the soul of the believer. Faith and love are quenched. The believer is now capable of committing voluntary disobedience against God, because the power of God has left him. Now he enters into sin.

Viewing these steps, it is clear that man does not abruptly enter into sin and then God departs. Rather man begins to toy with a tempting situation, and God begins to be crowded out. As long as we draw close to God, His power keeps us from sin. This is what John is telling us when he writes, "Whoever has been born of God does not sin, for His seed remains in him; and he cannot sin, because he has been born of God" (1 John 3:9). As long as we have God's presence abiding in us, we are kept from sin, but to grieve the Spirit of God is to open the door to voluntary disobedience again.

There are some key verses which plainly tell us the Bible standard for the born again Christian:

Everyone who sins breaks the law; in fact, sin is lawlessness. But you know that he appeared so that he might take away our sins. And in him is no sin. No one who lives in him keeps on sinning. No one who continues to sin has either seen him or known him. Dear children, do not let anyone lead you astray. He who does what is right is righteous, just as he is righteous. He who does what is sinful is of the devil, because the devil has been sinning from the beginning. The reason the Son of God appeared was to destroy the devil's work. No one who is born of God will continue to sin, because God's seed remains in him; he cannot go on sinning, because he has been born of God (1 John 3:4-9).

These scriptures can be understood only when one views them in light of John's definition of sin "sin is lawlessness," rebellion against God, a willful transgression. This then is the new birth demonstrated. Man lives in victory over sin, freed from the dominating power of sin. What a glorious state!

However, one negative note needs to be sounded. The carnal nature remains. In justification, the guilt of sin is cleansed; in the new birth, the power of sin is broken, but the nature of sin still remains. This subject will be seen in greater detail in another chapter. Here we must point out that condemning guilt comes not from the carnal nature, but from voluntary disobedience. Therefore, no one goes to hell due to the carnal nature or original sin. It is voluntary disobedience that brings judgment.

The question is often asked, How can Christ live within a person where sin remains? Wesley raises that issue and answers it in his sermon on "Sin in Believers." "'But can Christ be in the same heart where sin is?' Undoubtedly he can. Otherwise it never could be saved there from.

Where sickness is there is the physician 'carrying on his work within, striving till he cast out sin.' Christ indeed cannot reign where sin reigns; neither will he dwell where any sin is allowed. But he is and dwells in the heart of every believer who is fighting against all sin; although it be not yet purified."[14]

These considerations help us to see why justification and the new birth are called "initial sanctification." They are the beginning of a holy life. The Holy Spirit has made entrance into the spirit of man, but there remains the carnal principle.

Rev. H. Burwash explains that "the fundamental element in original sin" is not "original guilt but depravity, set forth as spiritual death; the new birth is not an absolution but a new life."[15] There is present within the believer the new life of the Spirit which helps to control the believer to a spiritual crisis in which God cleanses the heart.

I must hasten to present two great positive aspects of the new birth. They are adoption and the witness of the Spirit.

Adoption is reconciliation at its deepest level. It is sonship with all of its privileges. "For you did not receive the spirit of bondage again to fear, but you received the Spirit of adoption by whom we cry out, 'Abba, Father.'" (Romans 8:15). After the new birth we are no longer outcasts or slaves; we are next of kin to the Trinity. In Ephesians 1:5, Paul says that God "predestined us to adoption as sons by Jesus Christ to Himself, according to the good pleasure of His will."

This is not a passing whim of the Heavenly Father; it has been His heart throb from the beginning, God wants "to redeem those who were under the law, that we might receive the adoption as sons" (Galatians 4:5). Adoption speaks of freedom, fellowship, and acceptance. To the Roman society in New Testament times, it was a significant concept. One who was adopted was elevated to share equally with the children by birth. In this light, the "heirs of God, and joint heirs with Christ" (Romans 8:17) become of great importance to us.

Wiley writes: "Adoption is the declaratory act of God, by which upon being justified by faith in Jesus Christ, we are received into the family of God and reinstated in the privilege of sonship. Adoption...is concomitant with justification and regeneration, but in order of thoughts, logically follows them."[16] It is justification that removes our guilt. The new birth gives us the spiritual life of the resurrected Lord. Adoption brings us into the family of God as sons and joints heirs.

In adoption, all the privileges of sonship become ours. One of these is the witness of the Spirit. He who is born again has the inward evidence of acceptance with God. The Holy Spirit reveals this truth directly to the consciousness of the believer. Paul writes: "The Spirit Himself bears witness with our spirit that we are children of God..." (Romans 8:16). John tells us, "He who believes in the Son of God has the witness in himself..." (1 John 5:10). And in verse 6, John explains, "It is the Spirit that bears witness, because the Spirit is truth."

There is agreement among Bible scholars that the *witness of the Spirit* is twofold. There is "a revelation of objective truth and a revelation of personal standing."[17] Wesley lays a foundation for this teaching in his sermon on "The Witness of the Spirit." He points out that there is a witness of our own spirit and the witness of God's spirit.

The witness of our spirits is seen in a clear conscience when we view scriptural marks of a Christian. Some of these marks follow: "For as many as are led by the Spirit of God, they are sons of God" (Romans 8:14). "Now by this we know that we know Him, if we keep His commandments.... But whoever keeps His word, truly the love of God is perfected in him. By this we know that we are in Him.... If you know that He is righteous, you know that everyone who practices righteousness is born of Him" (1 John 2:3, 5, 29). And again, "We know that we have passed from death to life, because we love the brethren. He who does not love his brother abides in death" (1 John 3:14).

The list can go on and on. Conviction of sin, repentance, and awareness of the change from darkness to light, and the fruits of the Spirit are all good tests. Wesley writes, "Yet all this is no other than rational evidence, the witness of our spirit, our reasons or understanding. It all resolves into this: Those who have these marks are the children of God: but we have these marks: therefore we are children of God."[18]

When the witness of our own spirit is fully established, it is added to the witness of His Spirit. What is this witness? It is "an inward impression on the soul, whereby the Spirit of God directly witnesses to my spirit, that I am a child of God, that Jesus Christ hath loved me, and given himself for me; and that all my sins are blotted out, and I, even I, am reconciled to God."[19]

Wesley reasons well that the witness of the Holy Spirit must be antecedent to the testimony of our own spirit. It is necessary that we be holy of heart and life before we can be aware that we are sons. We cannot possibly know the pardoning love of God until His Spirit witnesses it to our spirit. So Wesley reasons that the witness of the Spirit must precede the love of God and all holiness. The experience of necessity must precede our inward awareness of it. The inner awareness is the witness of our spirits.

It must be plain that this assurance is more than an emotion or a feeling. It is a divine conviction which comes from the Spirit. This is important because the witness of the Spirit must not depend on feelings or the fluctuation of our moods. The reality of the new birth does not depend on feeling "Christian." Because our feelings fluctuate, we need the witness of His Spirit as well as the witness of our spirit. Each strengthens the other.

Every Christian who enjoys the witness of the Spirit seeks to give evidence of the marks of a Christian. The outward behavior gives credibility to others of our profession of an "inward impression of the soul."

In addition to the scriptures already cited in support of the new birth, one of my favorites is John 3. Here, Jesus is clear in His presentation to an educated man. Nicodemus was reported to be the third wealthiest man in Jerusalem. He had influence as a member of the ruling body among the Jews. He had been exposed to the best education of his day. At midnight he asked a question, "What do You have to teach me?" Convinced that Jesus was a teacher come from God, Nicodemus was ready to learn.

What is the constantly recurring truth that appears in the conversation? "You must be born again!" One soon becomes aware that Jesus is trying to communicate this fundamental spiritual reality to Nicodemus and to us. The new birth is His theme. It is a universal need. In verse 5,

Jesus says that no man comes into God's kingdom without this experience. In the same verse He explains who gives the new birth. Since it comes from the Spirit, born again Christians naturally grow in Spirit-likeness (John 3:8).

Another way to view the teaching of the new birth is through the process of questions and answers. In the introductory question Nicodemus inquires what Jesus has to teach him. Our Lord answers immediately, "Except a man be born again, he cannot see the kingdom of God."

This answer promotes further inquiry from Nicodemus. He asks, "How can a man be born when he is old? Can he enter the second time into his mother's womb, and be born?" Jesus replies that He is speaking in spiritual terms, not physical.

Nicodemus is still uncertain, and asks, "How can these things be?" Jesus then asserts His authority in the realm of spiritual truth. He gives an Old Testament illustration of Moses lifting up the image of a serpent which saved those who looked to it for help. His answer implies that the new birth is an operation of God received through faith.

We may also find in John 3 a series of contrasts between Nicodemus and Jesus. The first is human knowledge versus spiritual insight. Nicodemus has confronted Jesus and desires truth. Our Lord gives him deep spiritual insight into the Kingdom, but he cannot grasp it. Nicodemus questions, "How can it be?" Jesus then explains that a man could be a master of Israel and still not know deep truths about the kingdom of God. There is a wide difference between knowledge on man's level and Spirit wisdom that comes from God. Jesus tells Nicodemus He has come from heaven and will return to heaven. He has a source of spiritual truth that Nicodemus knows nothing about, although he has an opportunity to tap into the resource now.

The second contrast is seen as the conversation moves to biological life contrasted with Spirit-life. He has experienced a natural birth that operates on biological laws but Jesus speaks of a spiritual birth, that operates according to spiritual laws and gives a Spirit-life.

The third contrast presents death and perishing over against eternal life. When a man lives out of human wisdom only, he knows nothing but the natural life that ends in death. But when heavenly knowledge is communicated by the Spirit of God and an individual responds to that knowledge with faith, he is ushered into Spirit-life through the new birth. This is not length of days or extension of years but rather a quality of life that fits a man to live with God.

What a tremendous journey we have made! We have moved from total depravity to conviction for sin, to saving faith, to justification, and to initial sanctification in the new birth. We are reconciled with God. This reconciliation will widen and include areas of life unthought of at this point. Man is reconciled with God! He receives the Holy Spirit who is the Spirit of Jesus, and thus is enabled to live in harmony with God. Sin has received a deadening blow by the Spirit of God. Great things are being experienced and greater things are yet to come!

5

INCLINATIONS
OF THE FLESH

Entire sanctification cannot be properly understood
without the perspective of initial sanctification that
we have found in earlier chapters. There is a tendency
in some religious teaching and preaching to cheapen
initial sanctification. But we have seen that this glorious
experience brings reconciliation with God, which is His
design for man from the beginning. In conversion, sin
has been dealt a fatal blow, and one is no longer under its
control. When a deeper spiritual experience takes place,
it will be an extension of God's work already begun. Faith
is the response of man's heart that enabled salvation to
take place; any further work requires a response of this
same faith.

In the new birth man thus potentially receives from the
hand of God all that there is to receive. The power of sin is
broken, and one quits the sins of voluntary disobedience
against God. This enables growth to begin in the Christian
life. Jesus begins to teach His Word which brings new
light. Peace with God and the witness of the Spirit are
constant assurance for security.

It is at this point of new light that the need for a deeper experience begins to be felt; the light received reveals a hidden darkness not realized before. The Christian experiences a growing awareness that something deep within is not right.

Why has this not been seen earlier? Perhaps because all one could see was the terribleness of outward sin against God; now that that is gone, this real cause, the root problem, becomes evident. With a new determination one surrenders to Christ for the solution to all spiritual problems, beginning with this uncomfortable darkness which is so incompatible with the presence of Christ.

The problem comes to our attention in many ways. It may reveal itself as an inner pressure toward wrong. It may have shown itself in those unguarded moments when one suddenly reacts to a situation in an unchristlike manner. C.S. Lewis explains that as he came to his evening prayers, and reckoned with the day's activities, what bothered him most was those times he had "sulked or snapped or sneered or snubbed or stormed."[1]

If there are rats in the cellar, Lewis explains, one will probably see them if he goes in suddenly. Startling the rats does not create them; it simply allows one to see them before they can hide. It is the unguarded moment when the real make up of the interior life is revealed. We get to see ourselves in the sudden crisis and the quick reaction.

Initially the reaction is "Well, that is not the way I really am!" Agreed, it is not our finest moment, yet it is there. Or, "Well, that is just a natural reaction!" We must be careful not to fall into the trap of the modern-day evasionist who desires not to confront things but excuses himself by calling them natural or human.

Dr. William Sangster identifies this tendency in one of his illustrations. When the mother of *Tess of the D'Urbervilles* first discovered her daughter's sin, she said, "Well, we must make the best of it, I suppose. "Tis nater after all." That is what the spirit of the world is saying loudly today concerning a hundred different things. "It's nature and therefore hardly sin."[2]

But the Spirit of God will not allow that kind of rationalization. It may take some time, but He communicates the deep need of the inner heart of man. The rats will be exposed.

When the knowledge of this deep interior inclination toward sin is recognized and admitted, one is horrified. How can it be? The sin nature is worse than the sins dealt with in confession and conversion. The heart has become alive through the presence of the Holy Spirit. Through His eyes we see the nature of sin as worse than the symptoms (sins committed). It is the infectious condition that taints all of life, from which wrong attitudes and rebellious actions arise.

Discovering such a condition could beat one down in total discouragement, even making us doubt the possibility of being saved at all. But God is trying to help us; He does not want us to be defeated or discouraged. Wesley writes of awakened Christians in pursuit of sanctification. "And yet, for all this, they are not condemned. Although they feel the flesh, the evil nature in them; although they are more sensible, day by day, that their 'heart is deceitful and desperately wicked;' yet so long as they do not yield thereto; so long as they give no place to the devil; so long as they maintain a continual war with all sin, with pride, anger, desire, so that the flesh hath not dominion over them, but they still 'walk after the Spirit;' there is 'no condemnation to them which are in Christ Jesus.'"[3]

The condition in the inner person is one of turmoil and civil war. For a time the Christian may have been unaware of any problem and may have walked in utter delight, but now new truth has been seen. The soul is being prepared to enlarge its surrender and find a deepening of the present experience.

E. Stanley Jones writes, "The crisis of conversion brings release from festering sins, and marks the introduction of a new life. Conversion is a glorious release, but not a full release. Festering sins are gone, but the roots of the disease are still there. The new life is introduced, but it is not fully regnant. The old life is subdued, but not surrendered."[4]

Wesley says such persons "continually feel a heart bent to backsliding; a natural tendency to evil; a proneness to depart from God and cleave to the things of earth. They are daily sensible of sin remaining in their heart, pride, self-will, unbelief; and of sin cleaving to all they speak and do, even their best actions and holiest duties."[5] However, with joy he declares that at the same time they know they are the sons of God. They are deeply aware of His Spirit witnessing with their spirit, that they are the children of God. "So that they are equally assured, that sin is in them, and that 'Christ is in them the hope of glory.'"

There is no doubt that this is a state of new enlightenment where the deep inward carnal nature of the life is revealed. One with this knowledge is coming to a crisis moment where decision must be made. A clash of God's will and man's will is inevitable. The situations must find a remedy.

As one examines the depth of this problem, the focus falls on motives. Voluntary disobedience against the known will of God has been conquered, but there is internal strife between motives. Selfish attitudes permeate or taint good actions and thoughts. Jesus talked about this in the Sermon on the Mount, where He went behind the action to the thought process which produced it. Murder may be the terrible outward deed as far as the world is concerned, but it is the symptom of an inward hate according to Christ's teaching. It is the result of self-love. Adultery may be the terrible outward deed, but it springs from the inward lust which is driven by self-love.

It is interesting to see what has happened in this progression of revealed knowledge. At the new birth the life of Christ invaded one's spirit and delivered him from voluntary disobedience. His actions were not perfect, but he had a perfect motive. The intent of his heart was to do the perfect will of the Father. He was totally surrendered and walking in all the light Christ had given to him. But new light has brought into view a conflict in the spirit not known up to this time. It will demand further surrender to keep the motive perfect. In the midst of the struggle, one is brought face-to-face with a new crisis experience.

It is now clearly seen that the believer has two natures. The new nature imparted by God at conversion yields to the indwelling presence of Christ. Peter testifies, "by which have been given to us exceedingly great and precious promises, that through these you may be partakers of the divine nature, having escaped the corruption that is in the world through lust" (2 Peter 1:4).

But this glorious thought is clouded by the realization that sin dwells within the same person.

No wonder there is conflict within the believer! The new nature rises to conquer through the power of the Holy Spirit, who gives the resource necessary to live a victorious life, but the old nature is a constant spiritual drag upon the energies of the Christian.

What do we mean by "the old nature," which we sometimes refer to as the carnal nature? What is its essence? How can we identify it? What are we really talking about?

Wesley has been accused of referring to the carnal nature as a rotten tooth that must be yanked out. He constantly corrected this, however, by speaking of sin as a disease that the Great Physician must heal. Sin was darkness that needed the Light.

The carnal nature is not an object. It does not have physical substance. The tendency to deal with this spiritual disease in terms of a material substance sometimes causes confusion which we should try to avoid.

John A. Knight writes, "Because 'original' sin is not a material entity which in that case could never return once its roots were destroyed, the cleansing that occurs in a moment must continue moment by moment."[6]

John Fletcher also declared the need for Christ to guard constantly against the reappearance of the carnal sin of the heart. He illustrated it by a candle which must remain lighted to prevent the return of darkness.

Purkiser writes, "Depravity, original sin, inbred sin, or carnality by whatever name the fact may be described is best defined not as a thing, an entity or quantity... but as the moral condition of a personal being... one may say that original sin is more like disease, poverty, blindness, darkness, or the corruption of a severed branch than it is a root, a cancer, or a decayed tooth."[7]

If the carnal nature is not a thing, what is it? This should not be hard for us to discover. It is an attitude, a basic motivating disposition that feeds and encourages all wrong living.

What is this warped attitude? It is *self-centeredness*. This fact must be kept clearly in mind. When the carnal nature is identified in other ways, it may cause confusion. Richard Howard warns, "When original sin is identified as an attitude of rebellion toward God and/or enmity toward man, it is...confusing 'results' with 'causes.' Man is not born with these attitudes and it is difficult to reconcile them with an experience of regeneration. Rebellion and enmity are the consequences of original sin and not that sin itself."[8]

The carnal nature is the urge to self-sovereignty. This can be seen in the original scene of sin found in Genesis. Here Eve was confronted with Satan's question, "Has God indeed said, 'You shall not eat of every tree of the garden'?" (Genesis 3:1). The woman was quick to defend God by pointing out that they could eat of all the other trees. This one was off limits because it involved death.

The devil insinuated that God had been holding out on her, for He knew that if she ate of this tree, she would be like God, knowing good and evil.

Up to this time Eve had been dependent upon God. God was Lord in her life. But now through sin a shift was taking place which would dethrone God and enthrone self. Man would become his own god.

When God sent Adam and Eve from the garden after

the Fall, He said, "Behold, the man has become like one of Us, to know good and evil" (Genesis 3:22).

This seemed to be supremely important to Eve, but what did it mean? Richard Howard explains: "This cannot mean to know the difference between good and evil per se, because such knowledge is indispensable to moral behavior. Rather, does it not mean to know (or presume to know) what is good or evil for myself?"[9] God had once been the determining influence in their behavior; now they were choosing for themselves. God had been their standard of right and wrong; now they set their own standard. God had been sovereign; now they placed themselves above Him. Self-sovereignty was the first sin, and it has been at the heart of every sin from that time to this.

I can quickly recognize I was born with this tendency and have battled it my entire life. My first tears were for myself, all self-centered. A baby thinks only of his needs, feelings, and desires.

Did I outgrow it? One would hardly think so. Before long I was hitting my sister for taking *my* toy. Was this a passing phase of life? No. My selfish attitude was still very evident at age sixteen. A car pulled up beside me at the stoplight, and the challenge was on. I peeled rubber off my tires, beat him to the next stoplight, and puffed out in pride while I did it.

We recall these scenes and smile because we have all gone through them. But the smile is erased when we suddenly realize we are adults and are still controlled by childish self-centeredness. Someone has said, "The smallest package in the world is a man all wrapped up in himself."

The self-centered person constantly tries to avoid admitting personal responsibility for sin. The Hollywood star Flip Wilson is famous for saying, "The devil made me do it." One must blame the devil, the next-door neighbor, or the carnal nature. Anyone or anything must be blamed for the evil in my life, but certainly not my "self."

Keith Miller speaks of the kind of honesty that is necessary to overcome this shame: "The reason we are disappointed in our actions is because though we consciously wish to be good we really 'will' our own self-satisfaction. And until our true willing (which is mostly unconscious) is redirected, we are trapped and don't know why."[10]

In initial sanctification one has become honest enough to admit and confess his sins before God. Now that increased light has revealed our carnality, we must confess a larger, more intense area of conflict self-sovereignty against Christ-sovereignty.

As one deals in honesty with the events of life, he is driven to confront this problem. The evidences of carnality might be listed as follows:

1. Self-justification — unable to accept God's will or His reproofs
2. Self-evaluation — power-seeking, pride, prestige
3. Self-indulgence — laziness, sensuality, creature comfort
4. Self-exaltation — when God's will seems to curb personal ambition
5. Self-exoneration — I am right; non dare contradict me[11]

At the heart of this list is self — self-centeredness.

One also discovers that the root cause of voluntary disobedience against God is self-centeredness. The cause of sins is self at the center of the life. One must have everything to his advantage. He thinks only for himself.

Anger of itself is not wrong. The ability to be angry is a God-given attribute. No one can look at the life of Jesus with any discernment and see a man without temper. What then has happened to make anger evil? The problem with temper is not temper, but self-centeredness. As long as no one crosses me, I am fine. But it is carnal to lose my temper when someone steps on my toes. The temper has become self-centered instead of Christ-centered.

The basic drives of the human body are not evil in themselves, but when self-centeredness controls them, they become carnal. The sexual drive was created by God and designed to be a part of the productive power of man's living. No one can think clearly and call it evil.

But there are horrendous problems with lust, immorality, and adultery. The problem can be seen in the philosophy of the playboy, based on depersonalizing the female. It is the willingness of the member of one sex to dominate and use the opposite member for self-centered gratification. When one takes a person of inestimable worth and value in God's sight and reduces that person to a functional object, it is sin. Adultery or fornication is not a result of love for another, it is love for self.

The self-centered carnal nature may express itself in marriage or before marriage, too. When a man simply uses his wife or the wife uses her husband, a person of worth and value is reduced to a functional object. *Agape* love at the heart of marriage is destroyed. Often the result is divorce, sometimes because one partner has found another individual who meets needs or performs functions better than the present mate.

Carnal selfishness, however, is not limited to the areas of anger and sex. When management views the laborer as a function rather than a person, mismanagement results. When the laborer views management only as a means to meet personal financial needs, he is self-centered. Even the church is not exempt from this insidious influence. When laymen become functional objects of use to the church instead of persons of eternal significance, we cease to be the church. When we cater to individuals simply because they can provide money, teach classes, or provide music, the church has moved out of the realm of Christianity. The carnal nature taking care of ME and MY interests is expressing itself in our collective life.

Self-sovereignty is at the root of so many problems that it must be dealt with. Dr. Jessop writes, "Man has a sinful nature. He is born with an inclination or tendency to evil. His heart is wrong; he prefers his own way to God's way. This depravity or disposition to sin affects every part of man's being, and it renders him unable by his own efforts to deliver himself."[12]

While we have dealt with the Genesis account of the Fall, we need to advance further into the Word of God to establish the scriptural concept of carnality. Let us look at the terms the apostle Paul uses to describe this depraved nature of man.

In Romans 6:6 we read, "knowing this, that our old man was crucified with Him, that the body of sin might be done away with, that we should no longer be slaves of sin." In Ephesians 4:22 he exhorts, "that you put off, concerning your former conduct, the old man which grows corrupt according to the deceitful lusts…" And in Colossians 3:9, "Do not lie to one another, since you have put off the old man with his deeds…"

In regard to the "old man." Wesley comments on Romans 6:6, "Coeval with our being, and as old as the fall, our evil nature: a strong and beautiful expression for the entire depravity and corruption, which by nature spreads itself over the whole man, leaving no part uninfected."[13]

In the Ephesians passage the nature of original sin becomes clear through a series of contrasts. The darkened understanding (Ephesians 4:18) is contrasted with "the life of God." "Ignorance" is set over against the truth that is in Jesus. In the Colossians passage, we again see a vivid contrast. Paul lists the works of the "old man": "sexual immorality, impurity, lust, evil desire and greed" (Ephesians 3:5 NIV). One must put off this "old man" and "put on the new man who is renewed in knowledge according to the image of Him who created him" (Colossians 3:10).

In Romans 6:6 Paul describes carnality as the "body of sin." This actually means that man's body is under the control and dictates of sin. The terms "sinful body" or "sin's body" might be used. It is because sin so dominates and contaminates the outer man that man's body is pictured as sin's own body. Sin expresses itself in and through the body until it is identified as belonging to sin.

If one follows on in the book of Romans, chapter seven presents the phrase "law of sin." Much confusion surrounds this chapter, but there is little question that the term pictures "an inward constraining power of evil inclinations and bodily appetites, warring against the law of my mind."[14] There have been many who explain this chapter as a description of the newborn Christian having to battle with the carnal nature. But Paul seems to be speaking of a man under the law who is trying to live up to that law by his own resources.

Paul continues in Romans 8:7 with another phrase describing this inward tendency towards wrong: "The carnal mind is enmity against God; for it is not subject to the law of God, nor indeed can be." In the previous verses Paul clearly states what he means by "carnally minded." It is walking "after the flesh" (Romans 8:1); it is "the law of sin and death" (Romans 8:2).

If one "walk[s] after the flesh," he is carnally minded because his mind focuses on matters pertaining to the flesh. The carnal mind constantly pressures in the direction of wrongdoings. This is the foreign principle of self-centeredness which wants to gratify its own desire. Wesley describes what it is to be in the flesh as "under the government of it."[15]

We have seen the biblical truth which portrays the inner corruption of man. This defilement must be dealt with. Redemption must go beyond the forgiveness of exterior sins. Reconciliation with God must be reconciliation at the deepest level of living; there must be reconciliation in the inward heart. It is here that the Spirit of God has brought us. The light has come; the problem has been exposed. We are now accountable for the truth communicated by God's Spirit.

6

FREEDOM IN THE SPIRIT

Man reconciled to God is our continuing theme, because this reflects the entire purpose of God for man. Sin must be dealt with in order for reconciliation to be accomplished. Finding sin in two different categories would naturally lead us to expect two crisis moments in God's dealing with it. Outward sins (voluntary disobedience against known laws of God) must be forgiven. The new birth is the glorious act whereby God forgives, justifies, and regenerates the guilty person. Sins are gone; guilt is removed; man has become an adopted son of God. All is at rest for a time, but new light begins to flood the life through the teaching of the Holy Spirit. An awareness of self-centeredness makes the newborn Christian deeply aware of the new problem he is facing. However, faith takes hold as the Holy Spirit draws the Christian quickly to a second crisis experience called entire sanctification.

It would have to be admitted that there are wide differences of opinion concerning this experience. All one has to do is to mention the subject in a Sunday School class. There will spill forth such a variety of expression that one wonders where they all originated! However, the other side of that coin is the fact that there is also great agreement concerning this experience. "All evangelical Christians hold that it is a Bible doctrine, that it includes freedom from sin, that it is accomplished through the merits of Christ's death, and that it is the heritage of those who are already believers."[1]

Let us look at the terms that are used in the holiness movement for this experience. *Entire sanctification* is a good place to start. And we wish to see entire sanctification in connection with initial sanctification.

Wesley believed that love is the sum of Christian sanctification. There is only one kind of holiness which is found in various degrees. Wesley notes that these degrees are distinguished by John as "little children, young men, and fathers." He writes that entire sanctification "does not imply any new kind of holiness: let no man imagine this. From the moment we are justified, till we give up our spirits to God, love is the fulfilling of the law; of the whole evangelical law, which took the place of the Adamic law when the first promise of 'the seed of the woman' was made."[2]

The Holy Spirit who cleansed our sins in regeneration is now going to purge our nature from sin in entire sanctification. The faith that responded to prevenient grace and accepted initial sanctification will now enlarge itself to embrace entire sanctification.

Let us look at the word "sanctification" as seen in the Bible. *Hagiazo* is the verb form; it is used 29 times in the New Testament. In the Lord's Prayer, the King James Version translates this word as "hallowed."

In Revelation 22:11, it is rendered "holy," but in all other instances it is translated as "sanctify," "sanctifies," or "sanctified." The verb means "to render or acknowledge to be venerable, to hallow." It also means "to separate from things profane and dedicate to God, to consecrate and so render inviolable." The word is a unique religious term, appearing almost exclusively in biblical Greek.

In the Book of Hebrews, Christ's death on the Cross is clearly pictured as a means of sanctification for the believer. Speaking of Christ, the author writes: "He who sanctifies and those who are being sanctified are all of one, for which reason He is not ashamed to call them brethren" (Hebrews 2:11). Elsewhere the writer tells us that God made sanctification possible for us by "the offering of the body of Jesus Christ once for all" (Hebrews 10:10).

There is clear connection between the atonement and sanctification. Kittel writes:

> Paul applies the concept passively rather than actively, speaking of the sanctified.... Sanctification is not a moral action on the part of man, but a divinely effected state,...Finally in 1 Peter 3:15 Christians are summoned to the sanctification of Christ...The presupposition here is that they are hagioi ("holy," see 1 Peter 1:16), so that Christ dwells in them as His temple, and will not suffer any impurity. Again, therefore, purity of heart is a condition of sanctification.[3]

Hagiasmos is the noun and is used ten times in the New Testament. The word occurs in the Epistles and is related basically to Gentile Christians. It is translated both as "holiness" and "sanctification." A study of these ten occurrences should convince one that sanctification is made possible in Christ, through the Holy Spirit. Sanctification through the Spirit is the living form of the Christian state. Kittel again says, "If atonement is the basis of the Christian life, *hagiasmos* (sanctification) is the moral form which develops out of it and without which there can be no vision of Christ."[4]

Entire sanctification is a life derived from the presence of the ruling Christ. It is much more than "do's" and "don'ts." This experience ushers one into a life of perfect love which naturally demonstrates itself in moral living. Selfless love becomes the controlling factor. It is an abiding condition in which Christ is Lord of my life; the Spirit of Christ is in full control.

From the moment the Spirit of Christ comes to us in the new birth, He begins His claim upon the self-will of man. The ultimate question becomes, Who is going to be in control? One cannot serve two masters. Either Christ will rule our attitudes and choices, or we cease to be believers. Thus sanctification becomes the presence of the living Christ cleansing man of the carnal self-centeredness and abiding in control over the life.

The difference between the sanctified life and the self-centered carnal life is almost unthinkable. My life was like an old, junk Ford. The windshield was cracked, the tires bald, the fenders rusted, the springs flat, and the upholstery torn. The engine ran on only four cylinders, while blue exhaust smoke spewed from the tailpipe. About all I could get from my carnal, self-centered life was fifteen miles an hour.

When the Holy Spirit came in entire sanctification, I was given a brand-new Cadillac! The upholstery was luxurious; the fenders were solid; the car ran on eight cylinders. To my amazement, all I had to do was get in, buckle the seat belt, and hang on. God not only gave me the car He took over the driving!

Are you going to chug along at fifteen miles an hour, disgruntled and cantankerous, hoping you'll make it? Or are you willing to switch cars and accept all the resources of God?

Wiley states, "We believe that entire sanctification is that act of God, subsequent to regeneration, by which believers are made free from original sin, or depravity, and brought into a state of entire devotement to God, and the holy obedience of love made perfect."[5] He further explains that contained within this one experience is the cleansing of the heart from sin, and the abiding, indwelling presence of the Holy Spirit. It is the Holy Spirit who empowers the believer for life and service.

In a summary statement Wiley says, "Entire sanctification is provided by the blood of Jesus, is wrought instantaneously by faith, preceded by entire consecration; and to this work and state of grace the Holy Spirit bears witness."

Christian perfection is another term used for this experience. John Wesley strongly advocated this biblical language, but one has to admit that it has been a problem term for many people. It is a biblical term, but "perfect," in our language, implies having arrived, being unable to advance further. Certainly this was not in the thinking of Wesley. In his *Plain Account of Christian Perfection* he writes:

Question: *What is Christian perfection?*

Answer: *The loving God with all our heart, mind, soul, and strength. This implies, that no wrong temper, none contrary to love, remains in the soul; and that all the thoughts, words, and actions, are governed by pure love.*

Q. *Do you affirm, that this perfection excludes all infirmities, ignorance, and mistakes?*

A. *I continually affirm quite the contrary, and always have done so.*

Q. *But how can every thought, word, and work, be governed by pure love, and the man be subject at the same time to ignorance and mistakes?*

A. *I see no contradiction here: "A man may be filled with pure love, and still be liable to mistake." Indeed I do not expect to be freed from actual mistakes until this mortal puts on immortality. I believe this to be a natural consequence of the soul's dwelling in flesh and blood. For we can not now think at all, but by the mediation of those bodily organs which suffered equally with the rest of our frame. And hence we can not avoid sometimes thinking wrong till this corruptible shall have put on incorruption.*[6]

Our understanding of Christian perfection excludes *absolute perfection, perfectionism,* or *sinless perfection.* These terms refer to a state where there is no further room for expansion or increase of knowledge. Growth toward maturity is eliminated. But this is not the concept of Christian perfection.

In the New Testament the word *teleios* is often translated "perfection" and is used nineteen times. It means "whole," "complete," or "total." The perfect man is one who is experiencing the love of God spread abroad in his heart. He is living in full obedience to the will of God. His motives were purified in the experience of entire sanctification. Sanctification is thus a crisis experience which brings one to a state of purified motives, producing total obedience to the will of Christ. Kittel writes, "One does not find in the New Testament any understanding of the objective in terms of a gradual advance of the Christian to moral perfection nor in terms of a two-graded ideal of ethical perfection. Totality is demanded of the Christian in acts, too."[7]

There is a sense in which the concept of perfection can be applied to every moment of Christian endeavor. A newborn Christian must walk totally in all the light he has received. As new light is revealed, the area of his obedience is enlarged and his behavior becomes more nearly Christlike. In the midst of this increasing capacity, a revelation of the inner carnal self shows us the need for a crisis act of God to cleanse. Sanctification begins with initial sanctification and continues in growth, but there must come the moment of entire sanctification a crisis and instantaneous resulting in Christian perfection.

(1) Sin is (a) an act, (b) a condition, but (c) not an infirmity of body or mind it is a defect of love.

(2) Perfection is not absolute but relative that of a man.

(3) Perfection involves cessation from inward and outward sin.

(4) The Bible nowhere states that the body is essentially sinful and that deliverance from sin is impossible until death.

(5) The New Testament does state that deliverance from sin is possible and to be sought (2 Corinthians 7:1; 1 Thessalonians 5:23).

(6) The New Testament exhorts Christians to be like God in holiness and love (e.g. Matthew 5:48; John 17:17-21; 1 Peter 1:15).

(7) Christian maturity and completeness in love is the ideal for present realization in the New Testament (e.g. 1 John 4:12).

(8) Present justification is the condition of entire sanctification and the latter is the condition of final justification.[8]

Another term which can give us insight into this great experience is "perfect love," directly related to Christian perfection. Adam was created perfect. He had a mind that could perfectly know the will of God. He was provided with a perfect body that could do the will of God. For him perfection was perfect obedience to the perfect will of God as given to him. It was a standard of works. But Adam fell and consequently another standard had to be found by which man could walk in fellowship with God. The standard then became the heart motive. This was the only area in which man could be perfect. "Christian perfection is not a perfect living of life, but a perfect fountain from which the life flows."[9]

Love is the proof of discipleship. Christ states in John 13:35, "By this all will know that you are My disciples, if you have love for one another." Love is the fulfillment of being Christlike. Jesus himself makes it clear: "This is My commandment, that you love one another as I have loved you" (John 15:12). His love was perfect love.

Paul writes, "But above all these things put on love, which is the bond of perfection" (Colossians 3:14). John also plainly states, "And we have known and believed the love that God has for us. God is love, and he who abides in love abides in God, and God in him" (1 John 4:16). Galatians 5:14 tells us, "For all the law is fulfilled in one word, even in this: 'You shall love your neighbor as yourself.'"

In Matthew 22:37-40, we read, "Jesus said to him, 'You shall love the LORD your God with all your heart, with all your soul, and with all your mind.' This is the first and great commandment. And the second is like it: 'You shall love your neighbor as yourself.' On these two commandments hang all the Law and the Prophets."

Summarizing Wesley, Outler wrote: "As faith is in order to love, so love is in order to goodness and so also goodness is in order to blessedness."[10]

Perfect love goes beyond fulfilling the duty of the law. It is not the legal minimum; it is the love maximum. Love ceases doing the least one can and still get by. Perfect love is love in action with delight. There is no doubt that this is a condition of the heart.

To some degree it is always present in the Christian. In the words of Harald Lindstrum, "It is clear that this love must be the same kind as that granted to man at new birth."[11] The difference between initial and entire sanctification is a matter of degree. After the experience of entire sanctification, there is "no mixture of any contrary affections: All is peace and harmony."[12]

We must be as specific as possible in describing the sanctification. If one claims too much for the experience, discouragement occurs, because an impossible standard is established. If one claims too little, the Christian lives beneath his opportunities and is in danger of losing his soul. We must seek to understand what deliverance the crisis moment brings and what God will do to help us on to growth and maturity.

Proper self-love is in accord with the teaching of Jesus: "You shall love your neighbor as yourself." Lack of a wholesome sense of self-esteem can be as major a problem as self-centeredness. Entire sanctification cleanses us from carnality self-centeredness but not from self. It is the bloated self, the self out of control, that has to be dealt the deadening blow. Self must be brought under the control of Christ, brought to servanthood, and brought to dependence.

It is the mastery of self-centered desires and selfish choices that takes place in entire sanctification. It is not wrong to want to be liked by one's peers, but that desire must not control us. To be concerned about our appearance and to dress well is natural, but that desire must not override more important values.

The unique characteristics that God has given each one of us are not wrong. Even after being cleansed of carnal self-centeredness, I am still me. This principle of variety of gifts can be seen vividly in the writings of the four Gospels. All writers were under the control of the Holy Spirit, and yet each book portrays the individual personalities of the author as well as the inspiration of the Spirit. Leslie Parrott writes, "Sanctification deals with the heart, not the flesh. If your hair is red, sanctification will not change its color. A Scotchman will still be Scotch and a poor man will still be poor even after they are sanctified."[13]

Sometimes the natural personality traits that we have received from God are confused with carnal tendencies. Delbert R. Rose quotes Joseph H. Smith as saying:

> *Perfect love is "compatible with many deficiencies if not defects"... Perfect love out of a purified heart is not therefore to be identified with, or to tarry for, a well-skilled hand, or a well-trained mind, or a well-balanced temperament, or a finished character. It is rather a quality of nature and spirit with which to work at the task of building character, improving one's temperament, mind and skill.*[14]

Nervousness due to physical or emotional problems is not an expression of the carnal nature, nor is anger in its proper place. The righteous anger of Jesus as He cleansed the Temple was not the expression of a carnal heart. And Jesus was angry for the right reasons when He healed the withered hand on the Sabbath Day and was criticized for it. Mark says, He "looked around at them with anger, being grieved by the hardness of their hearts" (Mark 3:5).

In 2 Corinthians 4:7, Paul pictures the treasure of the Holy Spirit as contained in our frail human vessels. He recognizes that we are like clay pots which are easily broken, or fragile pieces of kiln-baked pottery. None of us is very strong without God's grace. We have weaknesses, limitations, lack of judgment, and other problems that arise from personality or temperament. Wesley writes of entirely sanctified persons: "Even those souls dwell in a shattered body, and are so pressed down thereby, that they can not always exert themselves as they would, by thinking, speaking and acting precisely right. For want of better bodily organs they must at times think, speak, or act wrong; not indeed through a defect of love, but through a defect of knowledge. And while this is the case, not withstanding that defect, and its consequences, they fulfill the law of God."[15]

In another place Wesley states: "This much is certain: They that love God with all their heart, and all men as themselves, are scripturally perfect…but then remember, on the other hand, you have this treasure in an earthen vessel; you dwell in a poor, shattered house of clay, which presses down the immortal spirit. Hence all your thoughts, words, and actions are so imperfect; so far from coming up to the standard…"[16]

These human limitations are not faults in perfect love, but they are restrictions upon the perfect expression and performance of a Christlike spirit.

At this point a discussion of eradication and control will help us to better understand the teaching of entire sanctification. What is eradicated? And what must one live with but control?

In his sermon on "Repentance of Believers," Wesley taught that a Christian can bring the deeds of his body under control. He can resist both inward and outward sin. He can even weaken the enemies day after day; "yet we can not drive them out. By all the grace which is given at justification we can not extirpate them. Most sure we can not, till it shall please our Lord to speak…the second time, 'Be clean:' and then only, the leprosy is cleansed. Then only the evil root, the carnal mind, is destroyed, and inbred sin subsists no more..."[17] Leo George Cox concludes, "If to eradicate means the same as to 'expel,' to 'drive out,' to 'wholly cleanse,' then it is a valid description of Wesley's concept."[18]

If this is true, where does control fit into the Christian life? Does eradication place a believer in a state where temptation does not touch him? Is he like a garden so completely weeded that none can grow back? The answer is no, because the physical figure is faulty. We are thinking about human spirits and not material gardens. For our purpose here we must understand that it is the constant presence of the Holy Spirit in our lives who both eradicates and controls. When He fills us, all self-centeredness, all that is unlike Him, is eradicated. But there is also an element of continual control.

The key area where control must be exercised in the life of the believer is within the body drives. Many believers have been confused when they discovered these physical desires were not removed in the experience of entire sanctification.

Paul teaches us that the body is neither good nor bad; rather it is neutral. But the body is still under the curse of sin. For years it has been under the control of evil, and those patterns have left their imprint within the drives. The longer one remains in sin, the more the body is exposed to sinful practices, and the deeper the scars of sin will be. It is like driving a nail into a board. One can pull the nail out, but the hole will remain. The size of the scar will be determined by the size of the nail and how deeply it was driven. In Colossians 3:5, Paul urges us to "put to death [mortify] your members which are on the earth..." One must bring the appetites under the control of the Spirit of God. *They are not removed.* One must live moment by moment surrendered to the Holy Spirit and experience His power in controlling them.

One of the great scriptures that teaches the second crisis experience of entire sanctification is Hebrews 4. The writer presents a Bible promise: There is wonderful rest for the people of God. This chapter is contrasted with chapter 3, which relates that the Israelites did not enter into the promised rest that God had offered to them.

In chapter 4 the author presents three great considerations. First, the rest is for God's people, and it comes as a promise from God (Hebrews 4:9). It is the fulfillment of the gospel that has been preached (Hebrews 4:2). This promised blessing enables us to shape our lives after the pattern of God's activity (Hebrews 4:10). The Hebrews of old missed this rest through unbelief (Hebrews 4:11). But we have the opportunity to enter into and enjoy it: "There remains therefore a rest for the people of God" (Hebrews 4:9).

Does this refer to some experience that we shall realize in heaven? No. Heaven will bring the ultimate in rest, but that is not what the writer is discussing. All the way through the chapter, he is speaking in the present tense. He urges us to get into this experience now. His key word is *today*.

Might this passage refer to the rest one experiences in the new birth? No. Salvation is a rest from struggling to earn the grace of God. But this could not be the rest the author is writing about here because those addressed are already followers of Christ. In Hebrews 3:1 he addresses them as "holy brethren, partakers of the heavenly calling."

We must conclude that the rest he is describing is for the believer who should experience a second experience now, at this present moment. This glorious experience involves having "ceased from his own works." The believer is to push aside all self-centered striving, and through a rest of faith be filled with the Holy Spirit.

The author thus tells us how we may obtain the rest. It is simply "belief." The Hebrew forefathers missed God's plan because of unbelief. The door to this experience, now as then, is faith. "For we who have believed do enter that rest" (Hebrews 4:3). Faith in God, which enabled the believer to experience the new birth, is now going to enlarge to encompass a second experience a marvelous rest in our fellowship with God.

As he closes this section, the author speaks of laboring to enter the rest. Here he speaks the intensity of purpose, of heart's desire. The believer must present his entire being to Christ; there must be but one single desire and passion. To rest in God demands total consecration of my life to Him.

Another great description of the experience of consecration is found in Romans 12:1-2: "I beseech you therefore, brethren, by the mercies of God, that you present your bodies a living sacrifice, holy, acceptable to God, which is your reasonable service. And do not be conformed to this world, but be transformed by the renewing of your mind, that you may prove what is that good and acceptable and perfect will of God."

Paul is here appealing to Christians, because he, too, addresses them as "brethren." He calls upon them to make a total consecration, because this is what is acceptable to God. He admits that there is a bent toward sin that causes the believer to be "conformed to the world." He therefore appeals for a transformation which is described as a renewal of the mind. Such a transformation of our spirits enables us to understand and share in "the good, and acceptable, and perfect will of God."

There is convincing proof for present and instantaneous entire sanctification in the tense of the verbs used in the Greek New Testament. In the passage we have just dealt with, Paul urges his brethren to "present" themselves to God. The verb is in the aorist tense which indicates a single act not needing to be repeated.

The same truth is seen in Acts 15:8-9, where Peter is reporting his experience at Cornelius' house. He declares: "God...made no distinction between us and them, purifying their hearts by faith." The verb "purifying" is in the aorist tense which means instantaneously, a completed act.

Again in Romans 6:13 Paul admonishes believing Christians, "do not present your members as instruments of unrighteousness to sin, but present yourselves to God as being alive from the dead, and your members as instruments of righteousness to God." Here, too, the verb "yield" is in the aorist tense. The list of scriptures that support this truth simply goes on and on.[19]

It is persuasive to note the number of times that God calls His people to be holy or perfect. In 1 Peter 1:16 we read, "Be holy; for I am holy." In the Sermon on the Mount, Jesus highlights this teaching: "Therefore you shall be perfect, just as your Father in heaven is perfect." (Matthew 5:48).

The Old Testament also calls us to holiness. "And the

LORD your God will circumcise your heart and the heart of your descendants, to love the LORD your God with all your heart and with all your soul, that you may live" (Deuteronomy 30:6). This circumcision of the heart refers to "that habitual disposition of soul which in the sacred writings is termed holiness; and which directly implies the being cleansed from sin, from all filthiness both of flesh and spirit."[20]

Certainly the God who has called us by His prevenient grace to be like himself would see fit to cleanse us from all sin. If we have responded to that grace by faith, initial sanctification has become the glorious result of forgiveness and deliverance from the power of sin. We are reconciled to God. However, the born again Christian cannot continue to walk in the divine light without the deep hidden parts of the sinful heart being revealed. At this point the faith that looked to Jesus for initial sanctification enlarges to include entire sanctification.

Christ through His Spirit cleanses the heart of all sin. Dividedness, civil war, and struggle with self are over. Singleness of mind, purity of motives, and perfect love towards God and man now abide. We are reconciled with God at the heart level. We are free in the Spirit!

Wesley writes in a letter, "Oh insist everywhere on full redemption, receivable by faith alone! Consequently to be looked for now.... Press the instantaneous blessing; then I shall have more time for my peculiar calling, enforcing the gradual work."[21]

7

THE UNFOLDING PRESENCE OF CHRIST

In the doctrine of entire sanctification it is possible to emphasize the crisis moment so exclusively that sanctification becomes only an experience in a moment of time, and "it" to be obtained.

John Fletcher, contemporary of Wesley, spoke strongly against this notion. He was fearful lest Christians consider sanctification "a state where we are unalterably fixed in his blessed favor, and forever stamped with his holy image; so that it matters no longer whether the tree is barren or not, whether it produces good or bad fruit; it was set at such a time, and therefore it must be a 'tree of righteousness still."[1] This would be a kind of false teaching that once we have been sanctified no more effort is called for, and we can never be lost.

However, there are many who have emphasized the gradual process of sanctification until they lost sight of God's gracious intervention. Consequently, sanctification has been thought of only as a gradual improvement brought about by one's reformation.

The truth of Scripture points to a balance between these two phases of the holy life. Wesley writes:

> *All experience, as well as Scripture, show this salvation to be both instantaneous and gradual. It begins the moment we are justified, in the holy, humble, gentle, patient love of God and man. It gradually increases from that moment, as "a grain of mustard-seed, which, at first, is the least of all seeds, but afterwards puts forth large branches, and becomes a great tree; till, in another instant, the heart is cleansed from all sin, and filled with pure love to God and man."[2]*

Wesley went on to insist that even this pure love to God and man increased more and more in order to bring us to "the measure of the stature of the fullness of Christ" (Ephesians 4:13). All sound holiness teaching insists on both crisis and growth.

No moment of sanctification is a cure-all. Reconciliation with God is a relationship that needs to be maintained on a moment-by-moment basis. Since walking with Christ is a relationship, we constantly need the help of the Holy Spirit. There is no point where heart purity abides in a static condition. Man void of God is immediately back where he started. The darkness is removed only as long as the Light is present.

In the sermon on "Repentance of Believers," Wesley preached:

> *By the same faith we feel the power of Christ every moment resting upon us, whereby alone we are what we are; whereby we are enabled*

> *to continue in spiritual life, and without which,*
> *notwithstanding all our present holiness, we*
> *should be devils the next moment.*[3]

His message was that we must lean on Jesus by faith, because from Him we "draw out of the wells of salvation." God is our Source of strength, enabling us to think, speak, and do what is pleasing in His sight.

It is this ever unfolding presence of Christ and ever growing revelation of truth that becomes the adventure of the Christian life. The longer we follow Christ the more we learn, and the more exciting we find the Christian walk.

It is also true that this growth is a process of correction. Entire sanctification brings to one's life a new center point, but it takes time for that truth to infiltrate his total living. For instance, patience is not all received at an altar. James tells us, "My brethren, count it all joy when you fall into various trials, knowing that the testing of your faith produces patience" (James 1:2-3). Patience is a virtue perfected through trials and frustrations.

A young mother cried out that she could never live a holy life because she had four children, all under the age of six. She lived with emotional strain that caused her to become impatient at times. Is it right to be impatient? The answer is no, because impatience hurts ourselves and it hurts others. God wants to help us in this area, but impatience does not nullify what God has done in sanctifying the heart.

There is a spiritual growth which brings order to the emotional life of the Christian. Many persons because of childhood experiences or sinful behavior have so wounded their emotions that years of healing under the careful guidance of the Physician of the soul may be necessary.

In the experience of human love, growth takes place. The bride and groom may be perfectly in love on their wedding day, but over the years that love will mature and become deeper. Likewise, a perfect love for God is experienced at entire sanctification, but that love grows with the expansion of our knowledge of God. I suppose everyone who has been sanctified wholly has said, "I don't know why I did not discover this experience sooner!"

There is no end to the growth of knowledge that takes place in the mind of the believer. Paul tells us that in Christ "are hidden all the treasures of wisdom and knowledge" (Colossians 2:3). I am convinced that to know Him who is Truth will require my entire life in time and eternity.

Another area of Christian growth is expansion in ministry, being used in the Kingdom. A life wholly committed to God finds ways of serving Him. One experience of ministry then has the tendency to prepare us for the next.

Our sensitivity to the Holy Spirit also develops through growth. We learn to listen for His call, and quickly to respond. This fine tuning takes place only as the precision instrument of personality is responsive to God again and again.

The second work of grace cleanses our motives. Instead of divided love, we love God and "one another fervently with a pure heart" (1 Peter 1:22). However, our intellectual, emotional, and volitional responses must be improved. Geiger writes:

> *The areas of growth, then, in the sanctified life*
> *are functional and multiple:*

a. *The strengthening of one's pure love for God*

b. *The improvement of love's control over mind, emotions and will…*

c. *The steady perfecting of one's total external life in the image of Christ.*[4]

Can one expect sanctification to eliminate all temptations? If sinful desires are gone, how could one possibly be tempted? We know that if desire is still possible, temptation is possible. For those things for which one has no appetite, there is no temptation. Leo George Cox answers by raising these questions:

> *Must it be conceded that the "lust" or desire made attractive in temptation really is sin? Should one conclude that a "stab of jealously, or a mood of irritation, or a sense of pride, or a lustful thought" is sin in the proper moral sense? Can not a person distinguish between a "sense of pride" and consent to pride? Might there be a jealously in which that will participates, at least partially, as over against a "stab of jealously" occasioned by temptation? In the moment one is aware of the passion awakened in temptation, is he the possessor of "evil" because the passion is good?*[5]

The answer to these questions is not easy, but there must be a distinction made between the desire which appeals to the individual, and the consent of his will that becomes sin. It helps to remember that Jesus "was in all points tempted as we are, yet without sin" (Hebrews 4:15). If He was truly tempted as we are, there must have been desire. But there is a difference between a momentary impulse, and the fixed position of the spirit in that "a soul may be so completely dead to sin and alive to God, that however attractive the object of evil may be to nature, the soul will have no corresponding movement toward it. The natural appetite or passion may feel that blind impulse, but the moral nature feels it not at all, but turns away from it with recoil."[6]

James writes, "But each one is tempted when he is drawn away by his own desires and enticed" (James 1:14). This verse must be investigated phrase by phrase. Temptation begins when man "is drawn away." No temptation can succeed unless it draws us away from Christ who is our strength and holiness. But note that man is drawn "by his own desire." Wesley says, "We are therefore to look for the cause of every sin in (not out of) ourselves. Even the injections of the devil can not hurt before we make them our own. And everyone has desires arising from his own constitution, tempers, habits, and way of life."[7]

It is at this point that man can be "enticed." The original word signifies "catching at the bait." It is evident that the basis of every temptation is found in the passions, instincts, drives, urges, and desires of the human nature. The sanctified heart must repel these temptations that come through natural desires.

To rightly understand the doctrine of holiness, we must remember that Christian holiness is more than the experience of entire sanctification. Being Spirit-filled and sanctified wholly is an indispensable part of God's plan for the Christian. But there is more. Holiness is a general term that relates to all Christian experience.

Initial sanctification is holiness begun. Entire

sanctification is a second crisis experience within the work of holiness. After the crisis, the Holy Spirit deepens and enlarges the scope of His work so that it encompasses newly revealed areas of the life. John A. Knight writes:

> *Holiness initiates and encompasses a divinely stimulated movement or process of grace and obedience, and extends from conversion to the final goal of glorification. Entire sanctification is a God-given moment or crisis of faith and covenant, which issues in increasingly responsible discipleship and immersion in the grace and knowledge of Jesus Christ.*[8]

Holy living requires consistent, total surrender. This surrender means walking in all the light that one has. It entails surrendering all that one knows about himself to all that he knows about Christ. A Christian cannot be less than totally surrendered to Christ and still be Christian. To refuse to obey Christ is to walk behind light. No Christian, whether born again or sanctified wholly, can disobey God and remain in fellowship with Him.

"No allowance is made or license given to love God with less than our whole being at any moment, or to love our brother less than ourselves, or to be walking behind light, or to fail to be spiritually minded. Nor are worldly mindedness and lukewarmness treated as innocent weaknesses which the Christian is exhorted to overcome gradually."[9]

Another area of confusion surrounds teaching on the work of the Holy Spirit. If one identifies initial sanctification only with the person of Christ and entire sanctification only with the Holy Spirit, he is wrong in his thinking.

We must not identify Christ and His cross only with initial sanctification because we have seen that the basis of the complete process of salvation is the sacrificial offering of Christ. The Holy Spirit is the Agent of that offering. He, too, is active in the complete process. Jesus teaches that the Holy Spirit convicts the sinner: "When He has come, He will convict the world of sin" (John 16:8). Titus 3:5 shows us that "He saved us, through the washing of regeneration and renewing of the Holy Spirit." Paul makes it clear that the Holy Spirit is at work in us from the moment of regeneration: "the fruit of the Spirit is love, joy, peace, longsuffering, kindness, goodness, faithfulness, gentleness, self-control" (Galatians 5:22-23).

The major issue at the moment of entire sanctification is not so much the believer getting more of the Spirit, as the Spirit getting more of the believer.

Nor does "the filling of the Holy Spirit" mean that the Spirit comes from outside the believer; that happened at the new birth. It means that the Holy Spirit who is already present and at work now receives the surrender of the rulership of life. When the believer releases his grip on the control of his life, the Holy Spirit fills his entire life.

It is exciting to see this truth reflected in the word *pleres*, used in the Books of Acts to denote "full of the Holy Spirit." The word literally means "rich fullness." The Holy Spirit who is already present is now seen in a new, rich fullness.

Richard Howard writes, "It is Luke who repeatedly speaks of being filled with the Spirit, and who exclusively uses another word for 'fill' (*pimplemi*), which has the basic connotation 'to saturate' and thus 'to possess' in a metaphorical sense. Furthermore, Luke always uses the aorist tense, indicating a crisis experience (cf. Acts 2:2, 4:31; et al.)."[19]

The symbolism is not that a cup that is empty and a liquid coming in to fill it; rather it is the picture of a sponge and the liquid saturating it. This beautifully depicts the fullness of the Spirit. Initial sanctification is the entrance of the Spirit of Christ into the believer. Entire sanctification is the saturation of the Spirit of Christ into the believer's life as He fills and cleanses him.

What an exciting picture of God and man reconciled in a growing relationship! It starts with the divine intervention called prevenient grace. As man responds and obeys, the crisis of regeneration ushers him into Christ's unfolding presence. But it becomes evident that a spiritual drag hinders the unfolding of Christ's revelation. A second crisis thrusts us forth like the firing of the second stage of a rocket. His presence becomes the guiding power and light. I am overwhelmed when I realize there is no end to the vast unfolding of His presence.

In C.S. Lewis' *Chronicles of Narnia* Jesus is pictured symbolically as the great Lion named Aslan. On their second journey into Narnia the children are in trouble in the forest. They finally escape for a moment and are asleep for the night. Lucy hears her name being called. At first it sounds like her father, but then she thinks it is Peter, one of her companions. Finally she realizes it is neither; so she stirs from her sleep.

She follows the sound of the voice, and then she sees Aslan. If it hadn't been for the movement of his tail, he might have been a stone lion. It had been several years since Lucy had seen him. She feels as if her heart will break if she waits one more moment. Rushing to him, she buries her face in the rich silkiness of his mane.

As she sobs, Aslan says, "Welcome, child."

"Aslan," cried Lucy, "You're bigger."

"That is because you are older, little one," he answered.

"Not because you are?" Lucy said.

"I am not. But every year you grow, you will find me bigger," Aslan said.[11]

I have found it true.

8

THE PRIZE OF THE HIGH CALLING

We have been on a journey so tremendous I have wanted to stop sometimes and catch my breath. The deep, sure flow of the Christian life is stupendous. It is the journey of a man who discovers God. But more truly it is the journey of God who finds the man. There are exciting crisis moments along the way. However, the real thrill of the journey is companionship with God and it will ever be so.

One man who captured the excitement of this journey was John Bunyan. He recorded his experiences in the allegory *Pilgrim's Progress*. Christian, the main character, is seen in the story as traveling on foot, which is how the Bible depicts our journey: "If we walk in the light as He is in the light…" (1 John 1:7). Paul tells us, "There is therefore now no condemnation to those who are in Christ Jesus, who do not walk according to the flesh, but according to the Spirit" (Romans 8:1). Something about walking allows deeper involvement in everything that is going on around us.

We started our journey with the awareness of man's

terrible fall into sin remedied by God's amazing prevenient grace. From the beginning to the end, God has taken the initiative. Man's awareness of sin in his life comes because God convicts him. Bunyan depicts Christian as a man with a horrible burden on his back. As he was reading a Book, an inward misery began to grip him until he had to cry out, "What must I do to be saved?" He must make the journey. Obstinate and Pliable, his neighbors, were of little help. Worldly Wiseman pointed out the unreasonableness of making such a trip. Yet, God was calling.

As one experiences God's call and follows it, not without difficulty, he will come to the experience of initial sanctification. While there is the tenderness of God's forgiveness, there is also the violence of God breaking the power of sin and giving new life. Bunyan shows Christian following the evangelist's directions (prevenient grace); he ends up at a little gate. Over the gate is written, in bold letters: KNOCK, AND IT SHALL BE OPENED UNTO YOU.

Christian knocks, but there is no answer. He knocks again and again. Finally he cries out. At last one called Goodwill comes to the gate. Upon discovering what Christian wants, he opens the gate, reaches out, and pulls Christian inside. Goodwill explains that not far from the gate there is a castle guarded by Beelzebub and his men. From it they shoot arrows at those standing by the gate, hoping to injure them and prevent them from entering.

Christian is then told that an open door is set before him, which no man can shut. The beautiful journey of the Christian adventure stretches before him.

As one makes the Christian journey, it becomes evident

that all things are not well. The hideous carnal nature residing in the inner man is seen in its true light. But God has made amazing provision to cleanse the heart through entire sanctification. This experience is seen in Bunyan's account of the "Horrors of the Valley of Death."

Suddenly, Christian is met by two men, Self-love and Critic, who are coming back in a hurry. They have horrible tales to relate of the Valley of Death. The spirit of self-love and criticism can never emerge from that valley alive. Christian, however, continues his way upon a narrow path which is almost like walking along the edge of a cliff, with a bottomless pit on either side. The horrors of inner sin attempt to stop him, but he hears a voice saying, "though I walk through the valley of the shadow of death, I will fear no evil; for You are with me ..." (Psalm 23:4). The awareness of the Spirit of God becomes his strength. The cleansing from his self-centered carnal nature and the filling of the Holy Spirit become his resource for the rest of the journey.

Beyond the Valley of Death, Christian has experience after experience. Some of them are difficult, some are enjoyable, but all produce a wisdom and maturity which comes from Christian growth. The Christian's progress is a journey toward wholeness.

The journey leads to the City of God. When Christian nears his destination, the reflection of the sun upon the city of pure gold is so bright that he can not look at it. When he comes to the gate, between him and the city is a deep river, dark and cold. There is no bridge. At first Christian begins to sink as he enters the river. But by faith he gets a good footing and makes it across.

Ultimate sanctification is the grand prize! The apostle

Paul desired it: "Not that I have already attained, or am already perfected; but I press on, that I may lay hold of that for which Christ Jesus has also laid hold of me" (Philippians 3:12). There is a perfection now but there is also a perfection that he had not yet attained. It is "the prize of the upward call of God in Christ Jesus" (Philippians 3:14). This is the resurrection from among the dead; this is glorification.

Holiness will climax in heaven. Here is the place where holy men go. The body which has lived under the curse of sin will be changed. The believer, along with all creation, is groaning for this transformation.

Dr. Richard Howard indicates four vivid metaphors which describe ultimate sanctification.

(1) The body of man will be "redeemed" (Romans 8:23). The redemption which has taken place in the spirit will also gloriously occur in the body of man. He shall be delivered from the curse of sin.
(2) Paul tells us that the resurrection will be an "exchange" of the body. An earthly body will take on that which has not been made with hands (2 Corinthians 5:1).
(3) According to 1 Corinthians 15:51-54 the mortal, dying body will become imperishable, immortal.
(4) This earthly body will be "transformed" as it is brought into conformity with "his glorious body" (Philippians 3:20-21).[1]

Ultimate sanctification is Christianity in completeness both within and without. Let us press on!

Come, let us use the grace divine,
And all, with one accord,
In a perpetual covenant join
Ourselves to Christ the Lord:
Give up ourselves, through Jesus' power
His name to glorify;
And promise, in this sacred hour,
For God to live and die.
The covenant we this moment make
Be ever kept in mind:
We will no more our God forsake,
Or cast His words behind.
We never will throw off His fear
Who hears our solemn vows;
And if Thou art well pleased to hear,
Come down, and meet us now.
To each the covenant Blood apply,
Which takes our sins away;
And register our names on high,
And keep us to that day. Amen.
— Charles Wesley[2]

Something great has been happening in my life as I have been involved in this journey. I have been moving from fragmented Christianity, bits and pieces, to a united hungering and thirsting for Christ. My heart has burned with an impatience to be totally reconciled with God. I did not initiate this desire, it came from the "Light which gives light to every man" (John 1:9). God's grace has sought me out.

When I experienced initial sanctification, I became aware that it was "of God the free gift." He has done the saving in my life. He alone could make me just in His sight. His creative hands began a project which can be accomplished only by a master craftsman. I became "his workmanship, created in Christ." It was the new life of the new birth.

While there was no flaw in His work, He was not finished. I found a flaw within myself never before seen or understood: "inclinations of the flesh." Oh, how horrible! Yet in turning my eyes on Him, faith revived and I entered into the "freedom of the Spirit" (entire sanctification). I was set free from the spiritual drag that would have ultimately destroyed me.

The growth that I have been experiencing in "the unfolding presence of Christ" has made me realize I am not completed. He is not finished with me. I have gotten a glimpse of "the prize of the high calling" (ultimate sanctification).

It is a great journey! To walk moment by moment in the power of God creates spiritual growth which is the delight of the believer. This movement toward total reconciliation in both mind and body is the uniting thread which ties together every element of the Christian experience.

Such is a Christian's progress. Such a man's wholeness when perfectly reconciled to God. Man is complete in Christ.

NOTES

Chapter 2

1. John Wesley, *The Works of John Wesley* (Kansas City: Nazarene Publishing House, n.d.), 6:63.
2. Ibid., p. 68.
3. H. Orton Wiley, *Christian Theology* (Kansas City: Beacon Hill Press of Kansas City, 1971), 2:345.
4. Wesley, *Works*, 6:512.
5. Ibid., 7:482.
6. Leo George Cox, *John Wesley's Concept of Perfection* (Kansas City: Beacon Hill Press, 1964), p. 32.
7. Wesley, *Works*, 7:482-83.
8. Ibid, pp. 345, 374.
9. John Wesley, *Explanatory Notes upon the New Testament* (Salem, Ohio: Schmul Publishers, 1976), 4:213.
10. Ibid, p. 230.
11. W. T. Purkiser, Richard S. Taylor, and Willard H. Taylor, *God, Man, and Salvation* (Kansas City: Beacon Hill Press of Kansas City, 1977), p. 30.
12. Wesley, *Works*, 6:508.
13. Leslie Parrot, *Renewing the Spirit of Revival* (Kansas City: Beacon Hill Press of Kansas City, 1978), p. 101.
14. John Fletcher, *Works of John Fletcher* (Salem, Ohio: Schmul Publishers, 1974), 1:141.
15. Mildred Bangs Wynkoop, *A Theology of Love* (Kansas City: Beacon Hill Press of Kansas City, 1972), p. 155.

Chapter 3

1. Wesley, *Works*, 8:57.
2. Ibid., p. 56.
3. Wiley, CT, 2:381.
4. Wesley, *Works*, 5.59.
5. Ibid, 7:337-38.
6. N. Burwash, *Wesley's Doctrinal Standards* (Salem, OH: Convention Book Store, 1976), p. 431.
7. Ibid., p. 447.

Chapter 4

1. Wiley, CT, 2:409-10.
2. L. M. Campbell, *Witness to the Doctrine of Holiness* (Kansas City: Nazarene Publising House, 1915), p. 13.
3. Wesley, *Works*, 6:71.
4. Wiley, CT, 2:407.
5. John Miley, *Systematic Theology* (New York: Eaton and Mains, 1892) 2:332.
6. Wesley, *Notes*, 4:218.
7. Carl Bangs, *Arminius: A Study in the Dutch Reformation* (New York: Abingdon Press, 1971).
8. C. S. Lewis, *Mere Christianity* (New York: Macmillan Publishing Co., 1974), pp. 139-40.
9. Burwash, *Standards*, p. 172.
10. Wesley, *Works*, 6:6-7.
11. Ibid., 12:239.
12. Cox, *Perfection*, p. 51.
13. Wesley, *Works*, 5:231.
14. Burwash, *Standards*, p. 122.
15. Ibid., p. 447.
16. Wiley, CT, 2:428.

17. Purkiser et al., GMS, P. 459.
18. Burwash, *Standards*, p. 95.
19. Ibid.

Chapter 5

1. Lewis, *Mere Christianity*, p. 164.
2. W. E. Sangster, *Why Jesus Never Wrote a Book* (London: Epworth Press, 1956), p. 60.
3. Burwash, *Standards*, p. 75.
4. E. Stanley Jones, *Abundant Life* (New York: Abindon-Cokesbury Press, 1958), p. 209.
5. Burwash, *Standards*, pp. 121-22.
6. John A. Knight, *The Holiness Pilgrimage* (Kansas City: Beacon Hill Press of Kansas City, 1973), p. 90.
7. Purkiser et al., GMS, p. 87.
8. Richard Howard, *Newness of Life* (Kansas City: Beacon Hill Press of Kansas City, 1975), p. 42.
9. Ibid., p. 43.
10. Keith Miller, *The Taste of New Wine* (Waco, TX.: Word Books, 1965), p. 23.
11. Adapted from Kenneth Geiger, comp., *Insights into Holiness* (Kansas City: Beacon Hill Press, 1963), p. 45.
12. Harry E. Jessop, *Foundations of Doctrine* (University Park, IL.: Chicago Evangelistic Institute, 1938), p. 10.
13. Wesley, *Notes*, 4:377.
14. Ibid., p. 380.
15. Ibid., p. 381.

Chapter 6

1. Wiley, CT, 2:441.
2. Wesley, *Works*, 5:488.
3. Gerhard Kittel and G. Friedrich, eds., *Theological Dictionary of the New Testament* (Grand Rapids: Wm. B. Eerdmans Publishing Co., 1978), 1:112.
4. Ibid., p. 113.
5. Wiley, CT, 2:466-67.
6. Wesley, *Works*, 11:394.
7. Kittel, TDNT, 8:77.
8. George Allen Turner, *The Vision Which Transforms* (Kansas City: Beacon Hill Press of Kansas City, 1970), p. 256.
9. Cox, *Perfection*, p. 141.
10. Albert C. Outler, ed., *John Wesley* (New York: Oxford University Press, 1964), p. 31.
11. Harald Lindstrum, *Wesley and Sanctification* (London: Epworth Press, 1946), p. 141.
12. Wesley, *Works*, 6:489.
13. Leslie Parrott, *What Is Sanctification* (Kansas City: Beacon Hill Press, n.d.), p. 29.
14. Delbert R. Rose, *A Theology of Christian Experience* (Wilmore, KY: Seminary Press, 1958), p. 163.
15. Wesley, *Works*, 11:419.
16. Ibid., 12:278-79.
17. Ibid., 5:165.
18. Cox, *Perfection*, p. 124.
19. John 17:17, 19; Rom. 13:14; 2 Cor. 1:21-22; Gal. 5:24; Eph. 1:13; Col. 3:5, 10-12; 1 Thess. 5:23; Heb. 13:12.
20. Burwash, *Standards*, p. 165.
21. John Wesley, *The Letters of John Wesley* (London: Epworth Press, 1931), 5:16.

Chapter 7

1. Fletcher, *Works*, 2:262-63.
2. Wesley, *Works*, 6:509.
3. Burwash, *Standards*, p. 135.
4. Geiger, *Insights*, pp. 102-3.
5. Cox, *Perfection*, p. 182.
6. Randolph S. Foster, *Christian Purity or the Heritage of Faith* (New York: Eaton and Mains, 1897), pp. 73-74.
7. Wesley, *Notes*, 4:589.
8. Knight, *Pilgrimage*, p. 11.
9. Purkiser et al., GMS, p. 510.
10. Howard, *Newness*, p. 157.
11. C. S. Lewis, *Prince Caspian* (New York: Macmillan Publishing Co., 1976), pp. 135-36.

Chapter 8

1. Howard, *Newness*, pp. 223-33.
2. Hymn written by Charles Wesley for the "Covenant Service." The first Covenant Service was held in the French Church at Spitalfields on August 11, 1755.

www.ingramcontent.com/pod-product-compliance
Lightning Source LLC
Chambersburg PA
CBHW061835040426
42447CB00012B/2978